Brian

The Life of a 20th Century Englishman

Brian Cookson

Published by Clink Street Publishing 2021

Copyright © 2021

First edition.

The author asserts the moral right under the Copyright, Designs and Patents Act 1988 to be identified as the author of this work.

All rights reserved. No part of this publication may be reproduced, stored in a retrieval system or transmitted, in any form or by any means without the prior consent of the author, nor be otherwise circulated in any form of binding or cover other than that with which it is published and without a similar condition being imposed on the subsequent purchaser.

*ISBN:
978-1-913962-55-5 - hardback*

*Dedicated to Susan, Richard and Sarah
and all the Cookson Family*

Acknowledgments

I wish to thank my daughter, Sarah and my son, Richard for spending many hours suggesting additions to and improvement of the text; and my wife, Susan for doing the final proofreading and editing and for providing so many of her photographs.

Contents

List of Illustrations   8

Preface   11

1. Birth and Parents   13
2. First Memories in Saltford and Trowbridge   15
3. Teenage Years in Worthing   27
4. National Service   47
5. University Years   59
6. London in the Sixties   73
7. Children and Move to Croydon   89
8. Retirement and Afterlife   103

Epilogue   127

List of Illustrations

1. Mummy with Me and the Twins
2. St Marys Church, Saltford
3. The three of us riding Rosie the Elephant at Bristol Zoo
4. Cricket at Elmhurst
5. My Bamboo and Ivory Mahjong Set
6. Trelawny's Cottage from the Walled Garden
7. St Mary's Church, Sompting
8. Dome Cinema, Worthing
9. The County Ground, Hove
10. Piccadilly Circus 1949
11. Forres Cricket Team 1948
12. Wellington College
13. Zube advertisement
14. Duke of Wellington
15. JSSL Crail dilapidated buildings
16. Foxton Hall Group Parade
17. Keble College.
18. New Theatre Oxford
19. Magdalen Bridge with Me Punting
20. Bridget and me on the Aldermaston March 1959
21. My Father
22. Delphi
23. Susan
24. Engagement
25. Cutting the Wedding Cake
26. Casino de Monaco
27. Grand Canyon
28. Richard and Sarah in Rochester Gardens

29. Fitzjames Avenue swimming pool
30. Me with chicken pox
31. Shirley Park Golf Club 3rd Tee
32. Letter from the General
33. Me in the Wooden Horse at Troy
34. Richard's Doctorate at York University
35. Sarah's Graduation a Leeds University
36. Mummy at an International Peace Conference
37. Blue Badge Guide Card
38. William Wallace Memorial, Smithfield
39. Discovering London Programme
40. Richard and Maria's Wedding with Parents
41. My Speech at the Bulgarian Wedding Ceremony
42. Sarah outside 10 Downing Street
43. China Socialism Slogan
44. Shanghai Locals
45. Susan at Xian with Terracotta Warrior
46. Sydney Opera House
47. Susan and me at Uluru
48. Christchurch Cathedral
49. Christchurch Cathedral after the Earthquake
50. New Zealand Suffragette Memorial
51. 30th Wedding Anniversary
52. Cooksons at Christmas
53. Big Ben at Midnight
54. Chinese Schoolchildren

All the illustrations are from Susan's photographs, Cookson family archives or Public Domain, except for those listed below for which acknowledgement for the permission to reproduce them is gratefully made:

Creative Commons Attribution Share-alike license 2 Neil Owen (2)

Brian – The Life of a 20th Century Englishman

Creative Commons Attribution Share-alike license 2.0
John Sutton (9)

Photo by Chalmers Butterfield (10)

CC BY-SA 2.0 Flickr user RTPeat (12)

historyworld.co.uk (13)

cc-by-sa/2.0 Copyright Jim Bain/Geograph.org.uk (15)

Creative Commons Attribution-Share Alike 2.0 Generic Steve Cadman from London, U.K (17)

© Copyright Andrew Abbott and licensed for reuse under this Creative Commons Licence (18)

Creative Commons Attribution-Share Alike 3.0 Unported license. tamara semina (22)

Laura Caillebot - Casino de Monaco Creative Commons Attribution 2.0 Generic license (26)

By Lennart Sikkema - Imported from 500px (archived version) by the Archive Team. (detail page), CC BY 3.0, https://commons.wikimedia.org/w/index.php?curid=73619388 (27)

By New Zealand Defence Force - CHCH City – Cathedral Uploaded by mattinbgn, CC BY 2.0 (49)

By Robert Cutts - Flickr: Tribute to the Suffragettes, Christchurch, NZ, CC BY 2.0 (50)

Mike Silver Photography (53)

Brian Cookson

Preface

I am not great or famous. But I hope my life has not been without some interest. It is true that as a young man I hoped to make an impact on the world. Like many youthful idealists I failed to achieve this ambition. Luckily this disappointment no longer bothers me. My favourite poem is Ozymandias by Shelley, about the great statue of an all-powerful Egyptian Pharaoh. It ends with these ringing words:

'My name is Ozymandias, king of kings:
Look on my works, ye Mighty, and despair!'
Nothing beside remains. Round the decay
Of that colossal wreck, boundless and bare
The lone and level sands stretch far away.

I also enjoyed reading 'Fame is the Spur', by Howard Spring. Few people remember this book today, but in the 1950s it was a compulsive read, relating the corrupting force of power on a man who started as an idealistic politician. It seems fame and power are not always the secret of happiness.

So, do not expect the fascination of looking into the life of a celebrity. But I hope you will find interest in the struggles, small triumphs, disasters and embarrassments of an ordinary middle class male. My life covers the period from the Second World War to the present very different world, although this book ends at the Millennium for reasons I will explain. Mark Twain famously said that the world had changed more during the reign of Queen Victoria than in the previous two millennia. I wonder what he would have said about the changes during my lifetime!

Before I begin, I have to say my memory is not infallible. I expect it is also selective. I have been as honest as possible. However I have never told anyone about some things which happened, and I do not intend to reveal them now. Surely I am not the only person who has some unprintable secrets? Other facts I have checked as far as possible with the people involved, although I take full responsibility for what I have written.

CHAPTER 1

Birth and Parents

I was born in a hospital in Trowbridge, Wiltshire, not far from the City of Bath, on 16th August 1937. That fact I am sure of, although of course I cannot remember it happening. This date is engrained in my memory which is just as well as today I am constantly being asked for the date of my birth by Internet service providers. I only wish I could also remember my passwords.

My parents lived in Saltford, a village halfway between Bath and Bristol. Their house was called 'Jeffreys Lodge' because the notorious Judge Jeffreys used to live there in the 17th Century. My father used to frighten me when we went into the coal cellar by telling me this was where the so called 'hanging judge' used to keep those he had condemned to be hanged.

My father, Claude Edward Cookson ("Ted"), was 58 years old when I was born. He had risen to be Governor of Sierra Leone, during the days of the British Empire. He did not talk much about this although he must have been an excellent horse rider. Several silver cups engraved with his name as the winner of races and Polo competitions adorned the side table in the dining room. My mother, Lilian Sybil Cookson, was his second wife and 21 years younger. Throughout my childhood it was she who was the most active parent. Her father, Norman Ulrich Holborow, owned a firm of cloth merchants called Collier. This was highly successful during his lifetime and he owned a large house in Trowbridge called 'Elmhurst'. So I have to say I came from a relatively privileged background. My parents brought me up in a traditional way for the time. Emphasis was on being useful, law-abiding, and a love of learning and sports. I will have more to say about each of them later. They were remarkable people in their different ways.

CHAPTER 2

First Memories in Saltford and Trowbridge

I remember nothing from before the war, which started just after I turned 2 years old. By this time twin babies - called Robert and Bridget, had arrived in my family. I have a feeling I was not too pleased to have my mother's attention diverted to the newcomers.

1. Mummy with me and the twins

I was mainly looked after by a Swiss au pair. I do remember being heartbroken when she had to leave because of the war starting September 1939. This was the first of the all too frequent disappointments in my early years in my relations with the opposite sex. After that, the first thing I remember happened on a sunny afternoon in early 1940 when we kids were playing on our lawn. Robert, who was quite stocky, was dashing around on his bottom. Then to my amazement, Bridget gradually got up on her spindly legs and started to stagger around upright. I told this story later at Robert's wedding, but he was not amused. I doubt if the date of one's first walk or talk is significant in one's later development, but sibling rivalry is prevalent in most families, I believe. Certainly it was true with us. I am ashamed to admit I used the fact that I was the eldest to gang up with either Robert or Bridget against the other sibling. Most shameful was the scheme Robert and I devised to trap our sister by putting books on doors so they would fall on her when she came through. The twins will have their own memories of these incidents, but I hope they have forgiven me.

Our village of Saltford was hardly affected by the war. I do remember being trained to put on gas masks, but we never needed to use them. Nearby Bristol was heavily bombed, but the nearest bomb to us made a large crater in the local golf course where my father played. We were allowed to roam there and later realised how lucky we were compared to so many other children who were evacuated. Rationing during the war affected the whole country, but we kept hens so had a decent supply of eggs which we kept preserved in a bucket of lime. We gave the hens names, and one was called 'Speckly'. I had rather ambivalent feelings when she turned up one Christmas for roast dinner.

2. St Mary's Church, Saltford

We were brought up as Church of England and every Sunday we attended the local Parish Church, which is very old, dating originally from Saxon times. We went with my mother. My father never came and I dared not ask him why. The idea of not believing in God never entered my head at the time. The main thing I remember about church was the irresistible urge I felt to look round to see the rest of the congregation. This was frowned on.

As well as regular churchgoing, we were encouraged to take an interest in nature. Picking blackberries and mushrooms were common ventures. We learnt how to distinguish mushrooms from toadstools, and never suffered any ill effects as a result. Today I would never dare pick a wild mushroom now that my mother is no longer here to guide me. One scary event is engrained on my memory. We were walking with my mother in the countryside behind our house, which we could reach through a gate in the back garden. We reached a pond and looked out for tadpoles. Then we three children walked on a wall which stretched alongside the pond. My sister fell in -

possibly pushed in by my brother, or just by accident. None of us could swim at the time and I'm ashamed to say I did not dare jump in to help her. My sister could not stop herself staggering deeper and deeper into the pond. Luckily my mother heard our shouts and went straight in just in time to save her. That was my first encounter with the thought of death.

More tragic for us was when my mother called us all together towards the end of the war. We children were devastated to hear her tell us that our grandfather (Grampa) had died. He was the managing director and owner of a quoted company. We used to go over to visit at weekends and he chased us around, up and down the two staircases of his large house. We loved these chases, but our grandmother (Granny) disapproved, as she was worried about his health. Sadly she proved right in the end. This was one of the few times in my life when I cried my heart out. As you will realise, I am a rather reserved personality. I put this down to the fact that I was a sickly child (more on that later), and brought up in the war. Then it was the stiff upper lip which was encouraged. This I gather is no longer fashionable, but I am too old to change.

I started schooling at about four years old. This was at a private house where Miss Hulbert was the formidable teacher of just a few kids. Actually I think she must have been good as I soon mastered my times tables. These alongside my birth date I will never forget. I had to walk to the school every morning, which involved crossing the main Bristol to Bath road. The traffic was of course nothing like as busy or as fast as today. But it was scary for me at such a young age. I do not think this would be contemplated nowadays.

Talking of transport, my greatest early adventure was towards the end of the war when I was 8 years old. I was put on a train at Saltford Station. This station was on the Great Western Railway, and had very short platforms. I remember the experience of being helped to climb up from the railway line to get into the carriage. Even today this would not be easy, but being so small made the carriage looming above me rather frightening. I then had to change at Crewe, which was a major railway junction, and catch the train to Chester in the North of England, near Liverpool, where my godmother, Jo Gaddum, met me. I stayed with her family for a week at Mobberley in the Cheshire countryside

The most significant event was the summer fete. At the end a banana was auctioned, a fruit which I had heard of but never actually seen. I cannot remember how much it went for, but this has always stuck in my mind. More recently I was amused to watch the scene in the TV series 'Dad's Army' when a charity fete is held in the church hall. Captain Mainwaring bids up and up for an orange being auctioned by the cantankerous fire warden, Hodges. This proved to be one of the few times Hodges came out on top, as Mainwaring finds he has bought a Seville Orange which proves far too sour to eat.

As I've mentioned, I was a sickly child. In fact at this time, before the MMR vaccine, it was considered beneficial to catch childish diseases such as mumps and measles. I caught the lot of them, except for Chicken Pox. That omission was to prove almost fatal later in my life, as I will relate in Chapter 7. I also suffered repeated bouts of tonsillitis and the advice was to have my tonsils taken out. For this I had to go to a local hospital run by nuns. The nuns were kind and offered me a cup of tea with sugar when I came round after the operation. This made me sick, and I have never liked sugar in tea since. I later heard from my mother that she had been horrified to be called to the hospital late at night to be told I was in a critical state and might not survive. Luckily for me I was unaware of this at the time.

One activity we enjoyed in Saltford was rowing on the River Avon. Mrs Poole, the owner of the local garage, used to take us out on the boat and teach us to row. Of course we could only handle one oar as they were very heavy. We learnt technical terms such as "catching a crab" (this happened rather often), and "feathering the oars". That was not easy with the heavy old fashioned oars we were using. Anyway it was fun to be messing about on the river, even if the experience did not lead to any mastery of rowing. I did later go to Oxford University, where rowing was a major sport. But there it was punting that I indulged in for reasons which will become clear.

Saltford is half way between Bath and Bristol, so visits to these cities were quite frequent and made a great impression on me. Our visits to Bath were to see the dentist. Having a tooth removed involved inhaling gas. This was probably quite dangerous, but at least it did not hurt. Much worse was having a tooth filled. There were no injections and the pain was excruciating. Today I complain if the slightest pain is caused after an injection and I am amazed we managed to endure the drill grinding into the raw nerve at that time. Whenever I think of those visits to the dentist I think of prisoners being tortured. I am ashamed to have to admit I would probably blurt out any secret if I was ever in that position. I have unbounded admiration for those who have endured torture especially if they managed not to tell their captors anything important. As a relief we also went to Mr Olsen's gym in Bath on quite a regular basis. I was no use at vaulting the horse, but learnt to climb a rope and do a crab on the floor. Another thing I will never forget is the Roman Baths. This was my first encounter with Roman civilization and it created a great impression. The strange atmosphere of the very green steaming water, surrounded by ancient columns, was awe-inspiring for my six year old eyes when I first saw it. Later I studied Latin, Greek and Ancient History for my 'A' Levels. This was nothing to do with my early experience with the Baths, but in later life I have always wondered at the presence of one of Rome's most impressive structures in our country. During the war the Baths were never very crowded and it was easier to appreciate their purpose than today when they are a major attraction with all the razzmatazz of the tourist trade. Little did I know at the time that 60 years later I would be taking coach loads of tourists to see the Baths, after I had become a Tour Guide.

3. The three of us riding Rosie the Elephant at Bristol Zoo

Bristol was quite different from Bath as it was a prime target for German bombs. I presume my parents were informed when it was safe to visit. We witnessed the frightening devastation of the ruined buildings and this imprinted on my mind the horrors of war. This had a big effect on my political activities during my student days. There were also real joys in visiting Bristol. One was visits to Bristol Zoo. Here we all rode on the famous elephant, Rosie. She was a former circus animal acquired by the zoo in 1938; she was very tame and gave rides on her howdah to thousands of children every year. This, together with a packet of Smith's crisps costing three pence, was a great treat. At Christmas time we went a couple of times to the pantomime at the Hippodrome. I remember climbing to the top balcony from which we watched Peter Pan from what seemed a great height. The story of the boy who never grew up, played of course by a girl, and his fight with the pirates, together with the "he's behind you" style of humour made for a great day out for us children. Today when I take my grandchildren to pantomimes they seem to concentrate much more on pop music than the story. For me the experience is disappointing compared with the excitement of the Bristol Hippodrome during the war. I am sure people will say this is typical of a grumpy old man and they are probably right. The most impressive structure in Bristol must be the Clifton Suspension Bridge. I seem to remember walking up to see it after tea at the historic Mauretania restaurant, which was owned at the time by the Avery family who were our neighbours in Saltford. However looking at the map of Bristol today I think it would have been too far for our short legs. It was and is a breath-taking sight. Last time I saw it was when the whole family did a tour of my childhood locations for my 75th Birthday. The Clifton Suspension Bridge was one of the inspirations for me to write a book about bridges as I will describe in Chapter 8.

Our time in Saltford came to an end after Grampa's death in the spring of 1945. Granny could not cope on her own in Elmhurst, her very large house in Trowbridge, with a garden and field stretching to over an acre. So my mother managed to persuade my father to sell up and we all moved to live with Granny in Trowbridge for about two years. This could not have been easy for my father as he never got on with Granny. They could not have been more different personalities. He was very active mentally and physically and intensely interested in politics. She was very religious, conservative and old fashioned. Fortunately I was too young to be much aware of this and my two years in Trowbridge between the age of eight and nine were among the happiest of my life.

4. Cricket at Elmhurst

We children were free to roam around the grounds. We played cricket and croquet on the lawns, and learnt to swim in Trowbridge's open air swimming pool. My father bought a new forest pony, whom we named Topper. He taught us to ride. The main problem was that Topper retained her wild streak and had a mind of her own. When she felt the rider was not in full control she bolted back to her stables and the rider had to fall off before reaching the low entrance or off goes your head.

My Granny employed a full time gardener, called Tom. He was an excellent footballer and we inveigled him to play with us, much to my Granny's annoyance. On one occasion he took me to a match when he was playing for Trowbridge Town. I remember nothing of the game. This was partly as a result of the shock when Tom took me into the players changing room after the match when I saw a group of naked footballers having great fun larking around in the communal bath. Needless to say, I was too scared to join in.

Summer holidays were spent at the seaside. Mainly we went to Weston-Super-Mare or Burnham-On-Sea, a short drive for us to the west coast and the Bristol Channel, where we loved the large sandy beaches and rock pools. Health and Safety concepts hardly existed in those days so we were free to swim and ramble as we pleased. Water has always been a source of pleasure for me, in all its shapes and sizes. But it also embodies a sense of danger. I remember walking out on the beach to the sea at Burnham when the tide was a long way out. As we approached the sea, sand changed to mud and there was a big dip. We were thrilled and scared at the risk of slipping down to our peril. The other resort we visited was Exmouth with its red cliffs. This beach was also sandy and the sun seemed to shine more than in other places. But my main memory is of meeting Aunt Agatha who was 86 years old. This was an unimaginable age for me at the time. I learnt that my father had 12 siblings, and she was the eldest. Later I was to meet the youngest, Uncle Geoff. We still have the table and chairs he left to us in his Will in our kitchen. Amazingly, none of them apart from my father had children.

After two years our stay in Trowbridge ended and we moved to Worthing on the South Coast. But I cannot leave Trowbridge without recounting my experience of two culinary delights. An elderly friend of the family used to come to tea, and he introduced me to milk-free China tea, with its more subtle flavour than common English Breakfast, which is an Indian tea. I have already related my less than happy first experience with the latter. Today I have grown to like Indian teas with milk for breakfast, but definitely no sugar. For afternoon tea I always have Lapsang Souchong. This reminds me of the games of Mahjong I used to play with the family friend after tea. I still have the set of bone and ivory Mahjong pieces which belonged to Granny.

5. My Bamboo and Ivory Mahjong Set

Even more of a treat for me was the discovery that a shop in Trowbridge sold Walls ice cream on Tuesday mornings. But it sold out quickly. We cycled into town early and usually arrived in time. There was either a vanilla bar for three pence or choc bar for four pence in old money. I recently watched a programme on television called 'Trust me I am a Doctor', where obesity was being investigated. The doctors warned that ice cream was one of the most addictive foods which led one to put on weight. This is because it contains both sugar and fat. This has not put me off as I love both sugar and fat, and luckily I can eat almost anything without putting on weight. However my taste for Walls ice cream was badly dented later in life when I met Unilever's chief scientist. I was teaching his team a new computer language, and over lunch he informed me it was made from whale oil and seaweed. I still love ice cream, but make sure it is made from real milk. The taste is just as appealing as with those war-time bars, but the excitement is not the same as when they were so hard to get.

CHAPTER 3

Teenage Years in Worthing

The move to Worthing took some time as my parents had to get two houses near each other so Granny could be looked after. They managed to find suitable properties in Sompting, a small village north of Worthing. One of the reasons for choosing this area was that one of my father's sisters, Aunt Dolly, lived in Worthing. I was sent on to stay with her and her companion, Lydia, while the house moves were arranged. It never entered my head that they might have been in a relationship. It may well be that they were just good friends. Nowadays it seems to be assumed that when two people of the same or different sex live together that they are sexual partners. As I will reveal later, I lived together with a male friend for two years. It was only later in life that I found out he was gay.

I stayed with Aunt Dolly for about a month. This was not the first time I had been away from my parents, so I suppose I had become fairly self-sufficient. However, I must have been lonely as there were no other children to play with. The main achievement during my stay was to learn bridge. This was before the Acol bidding system was developed, so the bidding was probably not very sophisticated. But the combination of skill and luck in the game has made bridge important throughout my life, thanks to Aunt Dolly. I have never been an addict, but it has been useful socially. Also it keeps the brain active in old age.

6. Trelawny's Cottage from the Walled Garden

After a month, the rest of the family moved to our new house in Sompting. This is called Trelawny's Cottage, after Edward John Trelawny, the former pirate who became a friend of Shelley and Byron. He lived in the house in the 1870s and died there in 1881. He sat as the model for the wizened old seaman in Millais's famous painting 'The North West Passage'. This was said to have been painted in the drawing room at Trelawny's Cottage. It now hangs in the Tate Gallery.

Much of the house dates back to the 16th Century and the fig trees in the garden were one of the reasons Trelawny bought the place. Unfortunately, none of us liked figs. One unusual aspect of the property was that it came with a large plot of land just across the road. This was used as a vegetable garden, and we were almost self-sufficient in fruit and vegetables for much of the year. The land was enclosed by flint stone walls, which are listed under English Heritage rules. The walls were very fine but were to prove a problem many years later when we wanted to sell the plot.

I was 9 years old at the time, and lived with my parents until I was 24, when I moved to lodgings in London. Much of the time I was away at Prep School, Public School, National Service and University. I will cover my most significant impressions of home and school life in this chapter in no particular order.

7. St Mary's Church, Sompting

Sundays we walked to church through a door in the wall at the back of our garden. This led to a twitten – a narrow pathway leading up to a dual carriageway which we had to cross to reach the church. St Mary's has a unique 'Rhenish Helm' style tower, dating to Saxon times. The rest is also ancient, but mainly Norman. The total effect is idiosyncratic and a bit of a mess from an architectural viewpoint. However, it is deservedly listed Grade I by English Heritage.

Two events remain in my memory. Once after service, we were walking down through the churchyard on the way back to our house. I stupidly told Bridget you could start a fire with a piece of glass in the sun. She tried it out and a hedge caught fire. As it was summer and very dry, we could not put the fire out. The Vicar came running down in his Cassock, not best pleased, but did manage to put it out. I do not think we told our parents, as they were very traditional and would have punished us. We were never beaten by them, but it did come close from time to time.

A happier experience occurred when I was learning the piano. The vicar allowed me to go into the church and play the organ when there was no service. I was shown how to turn it on and use the pedals and stops. I always admired the sound of singing with organ accompaniment in churches as it seems to reverberate more richly than in a concert hall. For me to actually play my favourite dramatic piece – Finlandia by Sibelius- in the empty church was thrilling. My musical talents are limited, but later in life I was almost as excited when taking part in The Messiah from Scratch at the Royal Albert Hall. This is when amateurs can perform Handel's Messiah, with professional singers. I found myself in the front row and to start with was cautious not to make a mistake. But when it came to the Halleluiah Chorus, I lost all inhibitions and belted out the notes as loud as I could. Luckily so did everyone else.

To return to our adventures in Sompting, we often walked or cycled up to the top of the hill to a copse on the South Downs. Here we played hide and seek before making a fire in the woods and cooking sausages and toast. Of course, this would not be allowed today. In a way we were lucky, living before Health and Safety and other rules were implemented. For example, I remember later driving back in my car from a summer dance in the nearby village of Steyning. I think I had company but was so drunk I cannot remember. Traffic was much lighter in those days, especially at nighttime, but I think I would have been in trouble if a policeman had caught me.

8. Dome Cinema, Worthing

There was no television then, so we spent a lot of time in one of Worthing's three cinemas, usually The Dome. For two shillings and nine pence (about 13 pennies in today's money), we could spend the whole afternoon watching the show twice. Normally things started with a 'B' picture which was cheaply produced, followed by the main film. I cannot remember any particular film but do remember one of the short feature films about the North Sea. This was repeated ad nauseam. At the end, the presenter said there was a plentiful supply of cod – and you know what you can do with that! This meant of course that cod was despised in those days. Sadly, our fishing fleet is now decimated and cod is as expensive as plaice.

We learnt to play tennis on the court on Granny's lawn. Uncle Luther, known as Uncle Chump, taught us. He had played at Wimbledon in his youth, so we soon became reasonable players. Sadly, he died being hit by a car when crossing the Sompting By-Pass. This was a great shock to all of us, especially to his sister, our grandmother.

We joined the West Worthing Tennis Club and cycled the two miles to the club most days during summer holidays. There we met many friends. For my age I was probably the best player in the club. One year there was a tournament for my age group. I reached the final to play against my rival, Alan. I stupidly was overconfident and was beaten, much to my chagrin. Later we were also rivals for the most sought after girl in our set. He won that battle too.

This leads me on to discuss relations with girls. I cannot remember having any sex education, and certainly the current approach to the subject, including transgender politics, would have blown my mind. We were all brought up in what would be called a Victorian fashion, so were naïve compared to today's youth. Going to boys only boarding schools also did not help. However, like any heterosexual teenage boy, I was increasingly drawn to the fairer sex. I got to know local girls, for example from the tennis club or friends of my parents. We were allowed to give dancing parties at our house and were invited out in return. These were chaste affairs compared to what I hear goes on today. Often foreign au pairs, working in Worthing, would come. I especially liked a German girl called Ute. I was delighted, if a little apprehensive, to be invited to stay with her family for a week in Essen. I was considered quite a good-looking boy. I even remember Ute's father asking me to take my glasses off and him saying 'selbst schoner' (even prettier). Unfortunately, my attempts at making advances did not match up, but at least we parted on good terms.

I will not bore you with my many usually unsuccessful flirtations. But I will always remember falling in love with a Dutch girl when Robert, Bridget and I went on a skiing holiday to a small village called Sedrun in Switzerland. Sedrun is one of the few places in Switzerland where they speak a language called 'Romansh'. Seemingly it is derived from Latin, but has words from Switzerland's three main languages, French, Italian and German. Apart from skiing and my affair, the highlight was attending midnight mass on Christmas Eve which I think was said in Romansh. Anyway, we met several people at ski school, where we were in the beginner's class. In those days, the skis we hired were wooden and heavy, which made our attempts at skiing rather clumsy. We eventually mastered the snow plough and then the slalom after a fashion. At the ski school, we made friends with a Dutch family, one of whom was the girl I fell in love with. My Dutch girl friend and I were devastated when we parted at the end of the holiday, but I had the consolation that her parents invited me to stay that summer. Her parents had rented a villa in Sedrun, while our parents had let us loose in a shared villa run by the specialist young person's ski company called Murison Small. The skiing experience was exhilarating for us all, and many future winter holidays were spent in the Alps. I had a great time in the Dutch family's home that summer and have many happy memories of cycling round Holland and visits to Amsterdam. I am not sure how you define love, but I am sure I felt it in Switzerland. Things were not quite the same in Holland, and the relationship ended. My now ex-girlfriend soon married a Dutchman. They both later visited my wife and myself and we still exchange Christmas cards.

9. The County Ground, Hove

Summers in Worthing were filled with visits to Hove Cricket Ground to watch Sussex. We used to cycle there and during the lunch break were allowed on to the outfield to play cricket with a tennis ball, while the ice cream and score-card sellers did tours of the ground. Large crowds watched the county matches then. My heroes were John Langridge and The Reverend David Sheppard. Sheppard was the most elegant batsman I ever saw. After a few years playing cricket for Sussex and England he decided to devote his life to the Church as Bishop of Liverpool. I understood that this was a noble choice, but as a Sussex supporter I found it very annoying. Frustratingly, Sussex never won the county championship during the many years we watched them, although they often came second. I rather lost interest in the championship after I stopped playing myself, until in 2003 I was thrilled to see that they were playing a match, which if they won, would result in their coming first for the first time I their history. I took a day off work to watch the last day of the match in the ground I used to know so well. Sussex won easily, and after the match the team streamed onto the outfield and did a lap of honour. The loudspeakers played the team song,' Good Old Sussex by the Sea'. Chris Adams, the Captain, stood in the pavilion to shake supporter's hands. When it was my turn, I praised him for surpassing the great teams I had watched before he was born. I think he smiled at that.

I must also mention another extraordinary cricket occasion. The final Test match of the 1948 England-Australia series was being played at The Oval, and this was to be Don Bradman's last match. He was my hero and my parents had bought tickets. The evening before, the Australians had just gone in to bat, so I was expecting to see him play when we were watching. He just needed to score four runs to take his batting average for Test Marches to an unimaginable 100. I was devastated to hear that he was bowled out by Hollies for a duck in the last over, so I never saw him at the crease. His batting average remained below 100, but at 99.6 is far the highest of any cricketer.

10. Piccadilly Circus 1949

Living with the sea to the south and the South Downs to the north we spent much time in outdoor pursuits. Until I moved to London in my twenties, I always considered myself a country boy. The first time my parents took us to London was soon after the war when I was 10 years old. I was stunned by our capital city with the flashing lights of the Schweppes advertisement in Piccadilly Circus and the scary experience of descending into the depths of the Underground on moving staircases. We had a four shillings meal in the Strand Palace Hotel, where you could eat as much as you wanted, and went to the Pantomime. Little did I expect then that I would later become a London Tour Guide and show people around the city sights.

Back in Worthing one of my fondest memories is of the cold winters when ponds froze over. We skated on the ice with no fear. There were no warning signs as there would be today. We also went to the Brighton Ice Rink, both to skate and watch Brighton Tigers play Ice Hockey. I never was much good at ice skating. I blame this on the old-fashioned boots they supplied. Today I am full of admiration for the celebrities who take part in the television show 'Skating on Ice'. I cannot imagine how they become so adept at pirouettes and other athletic maneuvers when I would have fallen over when just trying to do a turn. In general today I find the celebrity culture intensely annoying, but in this case I make an exception.

All the above activities occurred during school holidays as I was sent to boarding school from the age of nine. My father had been to Eton, and boarding school was considered obligatory for the middle to upper middle class of my parent's generation. My first school was called Forres. This was in Swanage, and I always remember my mother taking me in the car all the way to Dorset on my first day. I had been ill so missed the beginning of term. This meant that friends had already been made and I would be an outsider. I cried my heart out when my mother was about to leave me. She was probably almost as upset as I was but did not show it. Eventually I was handed over to a master and from then on had to fend for myself. In fact, my years at Forres were mainly fun. Friends were made, rivals fought but without violence, and sport encouraged.

Each morning we boys had to get into a large bath filled with cold water, and then drink a spoonful of cod-liver oil. This was unpleasant but I suppose healthy and meant to prepare us for any hardships of life in the future. The food we were given fulfilled the latter function without being healthy. I have an enduring memory of trooping into the school dining room each evening when trays of mugs, filled with green, yellow or red soup awaited us. We were obliged to finish our mug. As the mugs had been left out for some time after the kitchen staff had gone home, the soup was lukewarm. Worse still, flies settled on some of the mugs.

Our headmaster, called Mr. Chadwick, was a bluff character. We nicknamed him 'Chaddywhack', as he would give beatings to boys for certain offences. This did not happen often, and I don't remember being beaten myself. I do remember him calling us into his office when we were about to leave school to warn us against masturbation, which he said would make us go mad. The most feared master was Mr. McKay. I always think of him when I watch the television series 'Porridge'. Fletcher, played by Ronnie Barker, nearly always gets the better of the chief prison officer, McKay, played by Fulton McKay. This never happened with the real Mr. McKay at Forres. He was known for hitting a boy's wrists with a pencil of he got a sum wrong. He was a friend of my grandmother, and I came to respect his strict disciplined approach to learning Maths. Later I obtained 100% in 'O' Level Maths (equivalent to today's GCSE) and I have to thank Mr. McKay for this. I even use his name for some internet passwords. Today I have so many passwords I have put them in a password protected document. If I forgot this password I could be in trouble.

One of my proudest moments in the classroom was when we had a test in Ancient Greek. We had to decline all aspects of the verb 'Luo', meaning 'I loose'. I got it all right and was awarded the prize of a paperback version of Homer's Odyssey. Surprisingly, I found it an exciting read and it inspired me to take an interest in classical Greece. Later I was to study Greek, Latin and Ancient History for my 'A' Levels. This seemed an unlikely combination for the modern workplace, but I have never regretted this choice. I still have the paperback at home.

Having been introduced to Homer, I was then taken to a performance of Shakespeare's Macbeth in Swanage Theatre. Again, the story was gripping even if I could not understand all the words. So at the age of twelve I can say I was a fan of two of the world's greatest authors. Unfortunately, our English master, Mr. Farwell, was a fan of Dickens and forced him down our throats. I never liked Dickens until much later in life. Mr. Farwell was not popular. Apart from foisting Dickens on us, he used to take us on long walks over Ballard Downs. Then I would have much preferred to play sport, but today I would have been delighted to walk the Dorset coast. He did have one saving grace. This was his annual production of a Gilbert and Sullivan operetta, performed for parents during a long weekend. I can certainly appreciate the thrill of having a captive audience, especially when the applause is enthusiastic as was always the case with relatives attending. Unfortunately, I could not then sing in tune, so never got a major part. My last show was The Mikado. My best friend, David Lee, got the plumb part of the Mikado himself. I was one of the three little maids from school (of course all the female parts were played by boys). Funnily enough, later in life I went on a river cruise from St Petersburg to Moscow. One night we put on a show for fellow passengers and crew. Three of us rather tall men dressed up as the Three Little Maids and sang the famous song, 'Three Little Maids from School are We'. We just wore sheets and underpants. It at least raised a laugh.

It was compulsory to attend morning service in the school chapel. The headmaster was a Reverend and conducted the services. Towards the end of my time here I and several others were confirmed into the Church of England. On the day of the ceremony, the Bishop of Sherbourne presided. I had never met a Bishop before and was somewhat in awe. However afterwards at tea he turned out to be a jolly personality. I remember him being offered a second cake and his answer was 'I would if I could, but I can't'. I think this was the first time I met an important, although not famous, person.

11. Forres Cricket Team 1948

Sport and outside activities of all sorts was encouraged. We played cricket, soccer, and rugby, including matches against other schools. We also swam on Swanage beach, did athletics, went on long walks, and occasionally did boxing. The only sport I was quite good at was cricket. My best score in a school match was 71 not out against our main rivals, a school called Spyway. Rather surprisingly I achieved this despite forgetting my glasses which I was prescribed when it was noted I could not read what was written on the blackboard in class. In this photo I am in the team a year before I needed glasses. I had to wear increasingly strong glasses throughout my life until recently I had a successful cataract operation. Now I just need them for reading. They cost £1 at Poundland, which is rather cheaper than the £400 I used to pay for varifocal lenses. Much later in life my wife and I stayed in Langton House, which used to be where Spyway School was located. It has been turned into a holiday complex owned by the Holiday Property Bond, of which we are members. This of course brought back memories of my schooldays. We also visited my old school, Forres, which has now become a school for severely handicapped children.

In my last term at Forres I entered the exam for a scholarship at Wellington College. My father had been to Eton but found it an unhealthy location being near the River Thames. As I was a rather prone to colds and 'flu, he decided Wellington would be a better choice. Also he had been in the army and approved of the military association. Anyway, I have always been good at exams as I have an excellent short-term memory. I won a scholarship. I received a telegram from my parents with the words 'Congratulations, Well done, Love'. For some reason I have always remembered these words.

12. Wellington College

The start of my first term at Wellington was similar to that at Forres. I had been ill with 'flu and missed the beginning of term. This time I did not cry when my mother left me with my House Master at Stanley House. At Wellington, most boys stayed at one of the Houses who all competed against each other at sport. As at Forres, friends and rivals were soon established. No violent bullying took place as far as I know.

13. Zube Advertisement

However, I feel ashamed at how we all laughed at a boy with ginger hair and elongated face. We called him 'Zube' after the then famous lozenge with a horse on its advertisement. Boys, and I am told, girls can be cruel and do not fully realise the harm they do. That is until it happens to themselves. I personally had a problem later when I was nicknamed 'Mealy Potatoes', after a character in David Copperfield who had a pale complexion. One of the boys who teased me later went on to become a famous television presenter. He shall remain nameless, but at least he had the grace to write me a letter congratulating me when I obtained a scholarship to Keble College, Oxford.

The only actual violence occurred when masters or prefects gave a younger boy a beating. This of course is no longer permitted. I was beaten three times, for what were in my opinion harmless offenses. Once I was caught splashing another boy in the communal bathroom. The prefect who beat me was probably enjoying the experience as he achieved the record number of beatings in a single term. Boarding schools had a reputation for homosexual behaviour as testosterone develops in an environment where older boys mix freely with younger boys. I did not actually witness or experience any physical sex. But it was obvious when one boy fancied another.

Activities at Wellington, apart from the classroom, were similar to Forres. We did athletics and cricket in the Summer term. Again, I was reasonable at cricket as a slow leg-spin bowler. Many sunny afternoons were spent playing on the main cricket ground, with the possibility of visiting the school shop in the intervals. White ice-cream cornets were available for five old pence, and pink ones for sixpence. Parents provided a limited amount of pocket money for such expenses.

I did not enjoy winter sports as much, especially as if the pitches were frozen or too wet, we had to go on long distance runs of three or five miles. I usually ended up about last. Normally we played Rugby in the Autumn term, and Hockey in the Spring term. I exceeded at neither. For this I blame not being able to see without my glasses. Being a military inspired school, the Combined Cadet Force (CCF) was compulsory on Wednesday afternoons. I did not enjoy this. Especially unpleasant were the drills which took place rain or shine. Some boys were known to faint on hot days in the summer when forced to stand for long periods in the sun. I was pleased to be allowed to train as a radio operator towards the end of my school days as this got me out of some parades.

14. Duke of Wellington

The school motto is '*Virtutis fortuna comes*' which means 'Fortune favours the brave'. This was also the motto of the Duke of Wellington. I always rather admired him, probably from attending the school named after him. He is said to have remarked about his soldiers 'They may not scare the French, but, by God, they scare me'. He also insisted that all ranks should receive the Waterloo medal after his famous victory. I never became a great leader but like to think I would have behaved in the same way if I had.

One rather embarrassing parade took place when we lined the route for the Queen Mother on her visit to the school. We were supposed to cheer, but I doubt if she ever heard such feeble and intermittent noises coming from welcoming crowds. It was not that we did not appreciate her, but that we were all very English and reserved.

A year earlier Wellington CCF had provided a guard of honour lining the route of the funeral cortege of her husband, King George VI, to his burial in Windsor. The king had been an inspiration to the country in the War, and we were sad but proud to be at the ceremony. I had not known then about his speech impediment, as brilliantly portrayed in the film, The King's Speech. I did however know he had played in the men's doubles at Wimbledon in 1924 when he was Duke of York. Then he could not have expected to become King of England.

As at Forres, Chapel services took place every day. With over 600 boys and also teachers in attendance, it was an impressive gathering. I always enjoyed singing hymns when the sound of massed voices reverberates inside a church. Everyday services at school were part of my upbringing, and I had been brought up in the Christian faith. I did make friends with one boy, Naom, who was clever in a somewhat idiosyncratic way. Possibly he had a form of Asperger's, although I would not have suspected it at the time. He could read pages of a book by taking the whole in one go. He also read Proust's monumental novel '*À la recherche du temps perdu*' ('In Search of Lost Time'; earlier rendered as 'Remembrance of Things Past'). I have tried to read it but gave up after 50 pages. Naom was an atheist. This was an extraordinary opinion for me. We did not discuss this much at the time, and it was only later that I questioned my religious beliefs. In fact, at one time towards the end of my school days I became inspired by a Christian group I met. I discussed this with my uncle Arthur, who was a Church of England vicar. He encouraged me to become a priest. I seriously considered this. I suppose that if religion is true, one should devote oneself to God. However, life got in the way.

Wellington also introduced me to classical music, for which I am grateful. I had problems with singing in tune, even though I did enjoy singing hymns in church. When I was forced to do piano lessons as a complete beginner, my first lesson almost put me off, until my teacher played the slow movement of Beethoven's Pathétique sonata. The ethereal beauty of the sounds coming from the piano keys captured my imagination. I never became good at the instrument but was determined to learn the Pathétique. I can still play it today on our piano and am asking it to be one of the three tunes to be played at my funeral. One of the others is the Trumpet Voluntary by Jeremiah Clarke, which we played on the common room gramophone alongside 1950s popular music such as 'That's Amore'. I have yet to decide on the third tune.

The other skill I learnt at Wellington was how to dance the waltz, foxtrot and quickstep. Lessons were given by wives of the masters, some of whom were unsettlingly attractive. Those are the dances I am still most comfortable with. Rock 'n' Roll and Jiving were about to sweep the dance floors, but I was a late starter at all that.

I left school in the autumn of 1955, having obtained a scholarship in Latin, Greek and Ancient History to Keble College, Oxford. As a classical scholar and lover of classical music, I hardly seemed cut out for the modern world ahead.

National Service was of course compulsory then. However, students were allowed to delay it until they had finished their University course. I wanted to get it over with before going to University, so did not take up this option. Had I done so, I would have avoided it entirely as, unbeknown to me, National Service was about to end. So on a dark night in January 1956 I took the train to Darlington and on to Catterick to join up in the Royal Signals. Being unable to sleep in the crowded and uncomfortable British Rail carriage, I contemplated with apprehension the prospect of basic training with other young men who were unlikely to take kindly to a public school boy.

CHAPTER 4

National Service

I arrived at Catterick Station with a whole train-load of other anxious young men on a dark and cold January morning. We were bussed to the Royal Signals Camp buildings, interviewed and allocated to a billet. I think about 20 of us were housed in this long, low building and told we would all undergo basic training for two weeks together.

Immediately I arrived the professional soldiers, mainly corporals, mocked my accent. I admit I do have a somewhat posh accent. This would be known today as 'Oxford English'. In the past I would have considered the way they talked was rather common. I would certainly have thought they should try to speak properly like me. Here the tables were turned and I started to re-evaluate my attitude to different classes. It now reminds me of the famous class sketch where John Cleese, tall and patrician in appearance and demeanour, represents the upper class; Ronnie Barker, of average height, the middle class, and Ronnie Corbett, short in stature, the working class. Barker says "I look up to him [Cleese] because he is upper class, but I look down on him [Corbett] because he is lower class." Corbett replies 'I know my place'. In this case it was I who soon learnt to know my place as all the power rested with the corporals.

In the billet, I was also at a disadvantage with my fellow National Servicemen, none of whom appeared to be middle class. I suspect many middle and upper class boys had the sense to apply for the Navy or Airforce. I found out later that basic training there was less fearsome. Anyway, I did manage to get along in the end, as we realised we were all in it together. I do remember being shocked by their language. Every other word seemed to be some variation on the word 'Fuck'.

Having been to a boarding school, I probably found life in the billet less arduous than some of the others. But it was certainly tough. My main memories are of being assigned the task of cleaning out the toilets in our block, and peeling potatoes and washing up in the enormous kitchens. The food itself was no better than at Forres or Wellington. Coffee should have been a relief, but seemed to consist mainly of chicory, and was lukewarm. The rumour spread that the taste was also due to it being laced with Bromide. That is supposed to reduce one's libido, which might have been a good idea since there was no opportunity to meet girls during basic training.

One treat was an afternoon bus trip to nearby Richmond. This historic town could not have been more different from the grim buildings we occupied in Catterick. Some of us used our time there to visit the cinema, where we saw The Wizard of Oz. Today I would of course visit Richmond Castle, but then architecture and history were less attractive than light relief from our hard existence doing basic training.

This consisted mainly of keeping the billet tidy, especially making beds immaculately. Brass and boots had to be polished. This took considerable time as boots were hard with bobbles on the surface. These had first to be ironed out. Then hours were spent doing 'spit and polish' to achieve a brilliant shine. Of course after a day's basic training the shine vanished, and the process had to be repeated. Most of the time on active training was spent in various forms of military drill and marching. As I had been in the Wellington Combined Cadet Force, I had a head start over my fellows. I even managed to impress one of the fiercer corporals of whom we were especially afraid. He ceased to pick on me for my accent and we built up a mutual respect. I hope I have not given an unfairly negative view of the army in my account of this part of my service. They had an extremely difficult job to do, training us civilians in how to be soldiers ready to fight for our country. On the whole this was well done. One advantage the corporals had over civilian training was absolute power. Any insubordination was met with the threat of sending us to Colchester. This meant the Military Corrective Establishment which was an even harder experience for soldiers convicted of a variety of offences. Many violent men were incarcerated there and we did not want to join them.

I suppose I am proud of surviving this part of National Service as I was completely out of my comfort zone. The experience must have been similar to living under a dictatorship, although obviously not anywhere near as bad as Stalin's Russia against whom we were being trained to fight.

After the two weeks were up, we went on to different parts of the Royal Signals. In my case, presumably because I went to Wellington, I was considered potential officer material and sent to the War Office Selection Board (WOSB).

WOSBs were intended to select candidates who were capable of managing men. The Board took place over a course of three days, during which a battery of tests was used. We all lived together for the duration and built up a sort of camaraderie. We were given written exams testing our psychological as well as mental ability. At the end we underwent an interview.

The most intriguing part was when we were expected to demonstrate our ability to relate to others as a leader or in a more ambiguous position via Command Situations and Leaderless Group tests. As the names suggest, in Command Situations, a person was given command of a group whilst they completed an activity or held a discussion, and behaviour was observed by an examiner. In Leaderless Group tests, no leader was appointed to the group, who were then set a task to complete. The task was the "set" problem, but the "real" problem which psychologically trained observers were judging was our ability to balance the desire to do well as an individual with the need to work with and support other members of the group.

As any fan of Dad's Army will have seen, these practical tests could be amusing for the onlooker. Typically we had to cross an obstacle such as a river, using various implements provided, such as ropes, poles and barrels. In the case of my team not one of us crossed over successfully, and I myself fell into the river. Later it was explained what should have happened. This I suppose was obvious in hindsight. Needless to say, I failed to become a commissioned officer. I returned to the Royal Signals at Catterick and started training as a radio mechanic.

Having done only two terms of physics at school, I found the initial training challenging. We had to learn all about Ohm's Law and the various elements of a radio circuit, including resistors, capacitors and valves. Of course all that is irrelevant today, with advanced electronic technology. But at the time I was proud of completing the course. National Service provided many fortunate people a free training in a useful trade. I even used my skills later as a hobby, and built myself a radio which to my amazement actually could receive BBC programmes.

I remember very little of this part of National Service. The main events were the two times I was allowed home leave. This involved hitchhiking as I could not afford the train on my £1.40 a week. I would go to Scotch Corner on the A1 route to London and there wave down cars or lorries. Being dressed in uniform was a great help, as drivers were more likely to trust a soldier than a civilian. I had no difficulty in getting a lift. In those days hitchhiking was common. I myself picked up hitchhikers after I bought my own car, as I was grateful for the help I had during National Service. I did have trouble once when a man became aggressive and told me to go well out of my way for his destination. I managed to stop and luckily he got out. One hears of much worse incidents, which is a pity as hitchhiking is such a great idea.

I was about to start working as a radio mechanic, when I was called into see the Commanding Officer. He told me I had to go down to London to have an interview in the Ministry of Defence to see if I was suitable to train as a Russian Interpreter. This was my first and only experience of Whitehall. My father spent much of his working life in the Foreign and Colonial

Office, and my daughter, Sarah, now works in the Government Legal Department. I had always thought I would join the Civil Service as a career, but it did not happen.

On arrival at the Ministry, I waited with several other young men, feeling distinctly nervous. I always hate interviews. Watching the interview session at the end of the television series 'The Apprentice' brings back memories of many nail-biting and often disastrous interviews I have had. However in this case I was successful. My career as a radio mechanic was over before it had begun, and I was sent to Crail in Scotland to the Joint Services School for Linguists (JSSL).

15. JSSL Crail dilapidated buildings

Life in the camp at the small fishing village was bizarre. We were there to learn Russian, but also under military discipline. We took it in turns to do night duty. One of us was in command and we were supposed to patrol and guard the camp. The general feeling among us was that no one took this too seriously. On my night in command I let everyone sleep in the guardhouse. It was just my luck that this night a military policeman checked on us. I was court martialled in front of three officers. I had to wait under military police guard in an anteroom before going in for the trial. I admit I was scared as I had heard of what can happen at a court martial. In the past men have even been shot. Obviously if this had been any other military establishment I would have been punished severely for putting it at risk. Fortunately for me, it was decided just to give me kitchen duties rather than send me away, presumably as the forces did not want to waste their investment in my training.

As well as night duty we also had to do a limited amount of drill. This was conducted by a formidable character who insisted on being called 'Horse'. He had been a Sergeant in the Household Cavalry, where by tradition they are given the rank of Corporal of Horse. His parades were not unlike the caricature image of a ferocious sergeant-major screaming at his troops. He certainly had a witty and sharp turn of phrase. Typical would have been the following dialogue:

> Do you 'av a mother private?
> Yes Horse
> Was your mother beautiful private?
> Yes Horse
> THEN HOW, IN GODS NAME, DID SHE MANAGE TO PRODUCE A PIECE OF SHIT LIKE YOU!

Behind all the swagger we all felt he really was a lovely man, and the drill experience at Crail was far removed from the real terrors of Catterick. Students came from all three services. It was clear that those of us who came from the army had much the worse time of it in basic training. Also, naval candidates had been commissioned as officers before joining, whereas we were just privates.

The learning experience was intense. It is well described in the book 'Secret Classrooms' by Elliott & Shukman. The first eight weeks were spent in Crail, where we were taught the basics of the Russian language, including of course the Slavonic alphabet. Out of about 50 of us, 12 were to be selected to go to Cambridge to learn how to be Russian interpreters. The rest would do various Russian related work, such as listening in to Soviet military radio conversations. I was determined to go to Cambridge. I had been unpopular with some boys in my Sixth Form at Wellington as I was considered a swat. Anyway, my swatting ability did me no harm here. When the results of the final exam were put up on the board, I was amazed and delighted to see I had come top. This is one of my proudest achievements. Anyone who has read 'Secret Classrooms' will know that many of those who did the National Service Russian course had distinguished careers and some became famous. Among them were former Governor of the Bank of England Eddie George, playwright and novelist Michael Frayn, actor and writer Alan Bennett, dramatist Dennis Potter, and former director of the Royal National Theatre Sir Peter Hall. If I could come top here, surely I could go on to become a celebrity. But as the reader will have realised by now, this was never going to happen. So I have to be satisfied with this minor triumph.

The only relaxation I allowed myself during the 8 weeks was to listen to classical music on the gramophone in our common room. My favourite record was Schubert's String Quintet, with Pablo Casals playing the Cello. The rich, soaring tones of his Cello caught my imagination. It was that experience that led me shortly to buy a Cello myself. I was never very good, but could play slow musical compositions like The Swan by Saint Saens. Another pleasure was playing in an orchestra or String Quartet, where the ensemble sound is so much better than I could produce on my own.

There is always a feeling of regret when a group living and working together breaks up. However for the twelve of us at the top of the class, Cambridge beckoned. We could hardly believe our luck at being sent to University for a year as part of National Service. For us army students there was the added bonus that we were promoted to Officer Cadets, with a wage rise to £7 per week.

Brian – The Life of a 20th Century Englishman

16. Foxton Hall Group Parade

We were not considered part of the University, but were accommodated in a Victorian mansion called Foxton Hall, in the village of Foxton. Each morning we had to parade in front of the major who was in charge of the establishment. Instead of uniforms, we dressed in civilian clothes which had been issued to us. These we were allowed to keep after our service ended, but I have to say they were not exactly high fashion. Once a week we dressed in uniform to receive our wages. This was the only exercise which reminded us we were in the forces. It was far removed from Catterick or even Crail. The photograph shows us at the back dressed in uniform for our final parade. Our Russian teachers are sitting in front with the major in the middle.

One other event of military significance took place during our time here. The Egyptians under Nasser had nationalised the Suez Canal in October 1956. One day in November we heard that Britain and France had taken back the Suez Canal by force from Egypt. The Egyptians then blocked the canal so no ships could pass though. The Suez crisis of course proved to be one of Britain's most ignominious military engagements. Personally for us Russian students it was of course a relief that we would not be called to take part in any military action. A few days later we also heard that the USSR had invaded Hungary to suppress the Hungarian Revolution. These two events showed that the Cold War was still teetering on becoming hot, and that our interpreting skills might be needed in public service.

From Foxton we were bussed to Cambridge every weekday for the intensive Russian Interpreter course. Our instructors were a mixture of White Russians and Soviet defectors. Clearly they were motivated to ensure we learnt well. However there was no overt anti-Soviet propaganda. The formidable Professor Elizabeth Hill was in charge. She had instituted her own ideas of how Russian interpreters should be taught. This included installing a firm basis of grammar, weekly word lists for learning all aspects of Russian life, reading Russian literature, and of course pronunciation of the language. The idea was that we would be steeped in all things Russian.

The literature was amazing to me. I was especially inspired by Dostoevsky, and particularly 'Crime and Punishment'. This was not published in the USSR at the time as Stalin had much the same approach to books as Hitler, who famously burnt those of which he did not approve. Anything remotely against the atheistic Marxist state philosophy was banned, even if it was one of the greatest novels ever written by a Russian. We also had to read Soviet literature as this was more relevant to our course. 'Days and Nights', by Simonov, told the story of the German siege of Stalingrad. It was actually quite readable, although tarred with much Soviet propaganda.

Pronouncing Russian proved hard. This is largely because each word of more than one syllable has an accent. For instance, the Russian word for 'good' is 'хорошо' (khorosho). This has an accent on the last syllable and is pronounced roughly 'khara**shore**'. If the accent was on the first syllable, it would be pronounced '**khor**rasho' and the word would be meaningless. It is therefore essential to know where the accent is on every word. Although there are rules, there are many exceptions.

We had to record Russian readings and then have our pronunciation ruthlessly criticised. Towards the end of our year at Cambridge, we were expected to be fluent in Russian and speak almost like a native Russian. The USSR itself consisted of many nationalities, so there was not a single way of speaking the language. When I travelled there in 1958, a Russian I met took me for an Estonian – possibly as I had fair hair.

Later in the course, we were introduced to the strange technique of simultaneous interpretership. This means that the interpreter has to repeat in translation what is said two words behind the speaker. This was slightly easier to do when translating from Russian into English than the other way round. By the end of the course we would have all been competent interpreters if our services had been called upon. Fortunately, they never were.

The word lists were a key part of the weekly test. Anyone who failed two weekly tests running was likely to be 'Returned To Unit' (RTU). This was the stick which galvanised most of us to study hard. Two of our members did find themselves RTUed. One was sent away for supposedly 'refusing intransigently to pronounce Russian correctly'. I understand he later became chairman of a major corporation.

Out of the twelve who started the Cambridge year, nine of us passed out and were sent back to Crail to concentrate on military vocabulary and perfect our interpretership skills. At the end of five months there we qualified as Russian interpreters. Some went on to use the language in a variety of ways, probably some of them concerned with the Secret Intelligence Service. My son-in-law always pretends he suspects me of working for MI6, but my use of Russian was only put to use when I studied it for my Oxford degree.

During my time at the Russian course, two notable events took place. Having passed my driving test when I was 17 years old, I now had enough money to buy a second hand Morris 8, dating from 1937. This model was solidly built, but not as reliable as modern cars. I learnt to service it myself, using a grease gun to oil the underside machinery. The maximum speed was 40 mph. I used it mainly to drive back to Worthing on occasional weekend breaks. My best friend on the course, Dan Salbstein, also lived in Worthing and we travelled together. I had known him slightly before the course, and we still meet regularly. His rich deep voice was ideal for pronouncing Russian. On one occasion a tutor said he spoke Russian better than most Russians.

Even more significant from a philosophical point of view was my loss of faith in Christianity. This happened gradually as I found myself talking with many intelligent people who argued against religion. Eventually I came to the conclusion that there were so many religions that it was unlikely that any could be the only true one. However I remain deeply attached to Christian culture, and still like to attend Christmas carol services.

After I passed out, I was called back to another WOSB. My two years were now completed, so I was due to finish my National Service. If I passed, I would have had to stay on for Officer training to become commissioned as a second lieutenant. If I failed, I would immediately leave the army as a private soldier. I did manage to fail, although I cannot claim this was my intention. My leadership of the river crossing project was just as ineffective as on my first WOSB. But the clincher was probably my interview, when I expressed my admiration for Mahatma Ghandi and his campaign of civil disobedience. I cannot remember how this came up, but clearly the examining officer was not impressed. Promoting a pacifist-inclined intellectual who could not lead a group task was considered a bad idea. I have to agree they were right. In February 1957 I was released from National Service to return to civilian life. I dressed in my army issued trousers, shirt, jacket and tie and went home to my parent's house in Sompting.

CHAPTER 5

University Years

I now had to find some sort of occupation to keep me busy while I waited to enter Oxford University in September 1958. I was lucky enough to obtain a job as a junior travel courier with Swan's Tours. They were a family firm, famous for their luxury Hellenic cruises. They also ran cheap group holidays by train to Spain, Austria and Italy. The cost for two weeks on the Costa Brava was about £40 per person.

My job was to assist two professional couriers take up to 300 passengers from London Victoria to their holiday destination. The train took us to Dover, where we embarked on a Cross Channel Ferry – Eurostar was a distant vision at the time. We then took a special train from Calais which as far as I remember took us straight to our destination on an overnight journey. It was hardly the Orient Express, but at least no changes were involved. We couriers got no sleep as we had to help out at any time we crossed a border. This was before the borderless European Union existed. For instance, if passengers lost passports, 'special negotiations' with the border guards usually sorted the problem. I do not think we ever lost a passenger on my trips, but my colleagues had stories to tell of passengers stranded at Dover when missing the overnight train. On reaching the destination we had to bus the passengers to the correct hotel. Finally, we could go to our own accommodation and slump into bed exhausted. The upside was that we were not expected to help out during our five days in the resort as the local representatives took over. At the end of the week we took another group back to England. So I was paid £7 for two full day's work, and five days' holiday.

My main aim during the five days stay was to get a suntan to impress the girls. I have fair skin and the quickest approach was to lie on the beach until I got sunburn. This was painful, but after a few days my skin recovered, and I could turn a rather fine golden brown colour. I did not realise at the time how stupid it was to do this. I suffered for it later in my eighties when I had a basal carcinoma. This meant having on operation to cut it out and a skin graft from my thigh to cover the wound. There is now a deep hole in the back of my lower leg. I suppose when looking back this was a relatively minor youthful aberration compared to some of the mistakes I have made and later regretted. Anyway, my brown tan had some effect. One of the local representatives was a New Zealand woman who was a zany character. One night after we had all got drunk, she was sitting on my lap and said she could easily seduce me. Now I made a more serious error. I had been brought up to believe sex was wrong outside marriage. I failed to take advantage of her offer, which to a modern man must seem incredibly pathetic. Since I have brought up the subject of sex, I will now confess that I have never had sexual intercourse with any woman until I met my wife. In today's world I am sure I would have behaved differently. But at least I know I have not left any fatherless children.

My career as a junior courier with Swan's Tours ended ignominiously. After taking tourists to Spain and Italy, I was assigned the much quieter Austrian route where I was the only courier aboard. When I got to Innsbruck and took the passengers to their hotel, I found that Mr. Swan, Senior, was on duty as the local representative. When I tried to opt out of looking after the ongoing needs of the customers, which I understood was normal practice, he demanded that I carry on working. I was not about to forgo my "free" holiday and our relationship soured. He sacked me on the spot. Fortunately, this was towards the end of the season, and shortly after I went to Keble College, Oxford to study 'Mods and Greats'. This was the name given to Oxford University's prestigious degree in the classics.

Brian Cookson

The problem with doing two years National Service and then six months courier work was that my previously honed skills in Latin and Greek were distinctly rusty. After one week studying the boring texts of Cicero's letters, I gave up and opted for a Modern Languages degree in Russian and German. Russian was the easy part as having studied to be an interpreter I already knew the language better than would be required to complete the degree course. German however I had only studied from a self-taught Berlitz primer, so this would be a challenge. Unlike today's modern language students, we did not have a year studying abroad. Oxford University considered it beneath its dignity to teach the language as it was assumed we had learnt it at school. The whole degree course was oriented towards literature, history, and in the case of Russian, Old Church Slavonic. The latter has a similar relationship to modern Russian as Chaucer's English to our own language today. I could see no feasible use of learning it other than to pass the final exam. One benefit of studying this was that lectures were given by a young woman. She was much the prettiest of all the Oxford lecturers, not that there was much competition. We all speculated why she would want to devote her life to such a dead language. I did have one very embarrassing situation when I borrowed an ancient volume of Old Church Slavonic from the Bodleian Library. A fellow student wanted it and I agreed to lend it to him when I had finished with it. I did lend it to him without checking it back in first, but he never returned it, so I was pulled up in front of the Proctors (the University's disciplinary body). They suspected that I had kept it because it turned out that it was rare and valuable. Luckily, they were convinced at my clear amazement that they should think I had any interest in owning such a boring text. In the end I was let off with a reprimand. I could easily have been sent down.

There were exams at the end of the first summer (or "Trinity") term. This meant we had to study hard to keep our place for the full degree course. There were no exams during the second year. Many of us half gave up our studies during this time to pursue the many other attractive activities available. However, we suffered when the final exams loomed ahead in the third year and I think I worked even harder than I had done on the National Service Russian Course. In the end, I was awarded a Second-Class degree and can now call myself 'Brian Cookson, BA Oxon'. There was an option for Oxford BA graduates to apply for an MA by simply attending a degree ceremony. At other universities, apart from Cambridge, an MA is only awarded after further examinations. I never got round to applying, so am still just a BA.

As is well known, University is about much more than obtaining a degree. Living together with so many bright people opened up my mind and introduced me to a variety of activities. Out of these, I shall select some of those which had most effect on me.

17. Keble College

Oxford University consists of a group of colleges, where students live together. They form the basis of much of their social life. I went to Keble College, which is a Victorian building. At the time, Victoriana was rather despised, and I envied my future best man who attended the beautiful medieval Magdalen College. Today I have come to admire Victorian achievements in art and industry, and I find Butterworth's decorative red brick extravaganza appealing. My younger brother, Robert, who had cleverly avoided National Service, was already in residence at Keble a year ahead of me. He had stuck with Mods and Greats. One of his friends was a Hungarian man called Laszlo. He had fled Hungary after the Russians suppressed the revolution of 1956. He was an expert shot with a pistol and I believe he had killed a number of Russians before escaping to the West. Robert, Laszlo and I loved opera. We sat for hours listening to gramophone recordings of operatic arias, performed by great past and contemporary singers like Beniamino Gigli, Tito Gobbi, Maria Callas and Joan Sutherland.

18. New Theatre Oxford

We also joined the University Opera Society, where we sang works from famous operas. The highlight for me was when the Royal Opera House, Covent Garden, came to Oxford to perform Puccini's opera, Turandot, in the New Theatre. Several of us from the operatic society were asked to appear on stage as part of the chorus. I was made up as a 100-year-old priest. The sumptuous sounds of the singing and orchestra so near me were a revelation. I already knew 'Nessun Dorma', which is of course the highlight of Turandot. Much later this aria was immortalized by Pavarotti.

As regards social life, Robert and I were lucky that our sister, Bridget, was in Oxford at the same time as we were, at secretarial school. This meant that we met many of her female friends when there were relatively few undergraduate women. We partied and punted throughout the summer term. On one occasion, I made a mistake on the punt, which resulted in a girl called Gillian falling into the River Cherwell. I jumped in and rescued her. Luckily, this brave action impressed her more than my initial carelessness and we fell for each other. Some accused me of pushing her in on purpose to gain her attention as she was stunningly attractive. The relationship did not last the summer vacation as I had fallen for a Canadian woman I met on a National Union of Students visit to the USSR. I could not make up my mind which of these women to choose. I ended up losing them both.

19. Magdalen Bridge with me punting

Brian Cookson

Another event on the river stands out, known as May Morning. This starts early at 6 a.m. with the Magdalen College Choir singing a hymn, the Hymnus Eucharisticus, from the top of Magdalen Tower, a tradition stretching back over 500 years. I had booked a punt together with a female undergraduate who owned a flashy sports car. We and many others spent the night on the river and finally watched the ceremony from under Magdalen Bridge. For me, the view up Oxford High Street over Magdalen Bridge with Magdalen College on the right is the most inspiring in all the world. This is purely a personal and sentimental opinion, as I know that it does not really compare with world famous sights such as The Parthenon or the Great Pyramid.

Politics is often important to students, who are idealistic. We thought we knew how to make the world a better place. I remember having a curry with my Canadian girlfriend and looking round at our fellow diners as they chatted. I remarked how shallow their conversations probably were when we were discussing the great issues of the day. I plead guilty to this 'holier than thou' attitude. I find many of today's students who have this same feeling of moral superiority equally immature.

20. Bridget and me on the Aldermaston March 1959

My brother, sister and I had followed our parent's commitment to the Campaign for Unilateral Nuclear Disarmament (CND) when we were in our late teens. We all went on the Aldermaston March led by Bertrand Russel and Canon Collins. This ended up with a mass rally in Trafalgar Square. Looking back, I cannot believe how naïve we were as our desire for peace led us to believe the USSR was not so bad and the real villains were the Americans. Russia's brutal suppression of the Hungarian Revolution finally showed how dangerous the USSR was, and I ceased my membership of CND. However, my continued interest in politics took me to join the University Liberal Club. I became Secretary, responsible for finding outside speakers for our meetings. The president was Paul Foot, famous later as a radical left-wing campaigner and member of the Socialist Workers Party. We got on well until towards the end, when he started to show signs of disillusionment with the left of centre politics we liberals espoused. I remember having one fierce argument with him about what was the most important issue in politics at the time. I thought it was the need for our country to join the European Union. He was against this idea and insisted that Unilateral Nuclear Disarmament was infinitely more important. In later life I visited Highgate Cemetery, where Karl Marx is buried. Nearby the imposing Marx Memorial I found the tomb of Paul Foot, which brought back memories of our Oxford Liberal days.

One event stands out for me during my time as Secretary. Oxford is known as the home of lost causes and joining the Liberals fell into this category. However, when Jeremy Thorpe won the Torrington By-Election, this rare victory inspired us liberal students. I invited him to give a speech at one of our meetings and this proved the best attended meeting I witnessed at Oxford. I felt a real sense of pride as I introduced him to the audience to rapturous applause. Thorpe was charismatic and energetic, and we were bowled over by him. Little did we know the darker side which came out later when he was tried for murder. The 2018 film 'A Very English Scandal', starring Hugh Grant as Thorpe, portrays this with reasonable accuracy.

On a lighter note, I challenged a fellow Liberal to a drinking contest at one of our parties in Keble common room. Colleagues shouted encouragement to us both as we downed glasses of sherry. Finally I won when I gulped down my 19th glass. At the time I was living at Iffley, just outside Oxford and needed to cycle to my lodgings. I got as far as the cinema, but felt I had to rest and recover before completing my journey. I paid to sit in the cinema, but stupidly sat in the front row. On looking up at the screen, I felt violently sick and rushed to the toilets. I must have gone to sleep, as the next thing I remember was a stern voice demanding that I come out. I replied, 'No I will not come out so bugger off'. I received a shock when the reply came back 'No I will not bugger off – I am a policeman'. Shamefaced, I emerged expecting trouble. Luckily, the policeman thought it a bit of a joke and asked me if I was now capable of cycling home. This I managed somehow. Today I believe cycling under the influence of alcohol or drugs is a criminal offence, with a maximum fine of £1000.

During the vacations I did two fascinating journeys to Eastern Europe. I already mentioned the National Union of Students USSR tour. We went by train through Europe. Passing the East German border was scary, as the guards were armed and took an hour to check all passengers. One rather felt that the East Germans ran a more efficient Communist State then even the Russians. We spent two weeks in the USSR, visiting Moscow, Kiev (now part of Ukraine), and Leningrad (now St Petersburg). The overall impression was that life for the majority was grey. This was typified by the queues outside the huge department store in Moscow, known as 'GUM'. When people were at last served, the choice was limited or non-existent. This contrasted with the so called 'Beriozkas', which were foreign currency shops intended for tourists, as well as high ranking Soviet officials. The latter also drove round in large black limousines. The ordinary public did however have access to one of the most impressive underground systems in the world. The stations are constructed largely of marble and are tourist landmarks. Their photogenic architecture, large chandeliers and detailed decoration were intended by Stalin to show off the glories of socialist classical architecture.

In Kiev, we spent one evening looking for a restaurant which served anything other than meatballs for dinner. We failed. Leningrad was for me the most impressive of the three cities we visited. This was largely because of the architecture of the famous historic buildings, dating back to Peter the Great and Catherine the Great. Considering the devastation caused by the Nazis during the siege of Leningrad, the regime had done an excellent job in restoring the city. The massive St Isaac's Cathedral had sadly been turned into a museum of Atheism, which removed the feeling of awe which I had hoped for. Today the city has been renamed St Petersburg. When my wife and I visited in 2001, we were pleased to find the Cathedral was restored to Orthodox Christian worship.

A few of us students had a revealing meeting in the lodgings of a group of some Russian students. They played loud music which allowed them to say what they really thought about the Communist state. The music evidently drowned out any possibility of bugging devices being heard by the KGB. This experience gave an insight of how inhuman it must be to live in a totalitarian state.

The following summer my friend, Tim Bettany who owned a car, drove us around Europe, ending up in Hungary, Yugoslavia (as it then was) and Bulgaria. Yugoslavia appeared much more relaxed than the two Soviet bloc states. Tito ran a communist dictatorship but had broken free from Soviet control. In Belgrade we met a male student who clearly wanted contact with the West. He was very friendly and even offered to procure girls for us both. We declined, and he seemed disappointed with us.

Hungary was quite different. The hated Russians had invaded the year before to suppress the new democratic government led by Imre Nagy. After the invasion, they took

Nagy to Moscow, but then returned him to Hungary, where the Soviets had installed their own government. He was secretly charged with organizing the overthrow of the Hungarian people's democratic state and with treason. Nagy was found guilty, sentenced to death and executed by hanging in June 1958. We met a group of Hungarian students who took us to an island on Lake Balaton, not far from Budapest. After several drinks and anti-Soviet jokes, it was agreed that they would sing some Hungarian songs, if we agreed to sing some English ones. Their voices sounded majestic over the water of the lake. Sadly our efforts at singing Rule Britannia were embarrassing. 'Null Points' again for the British.

In Bulgaria we were introduced to a woman who had met my mother the year before, when she had been on a woman's peace convoy to Eastern Europe organised by Dora Russell, wife of Bertrand Russell. My mother was dedicated to the Peace movement but found many of her fellow travellers fanatically pro Communist and unwilling to see that the Soviet bloc was profoundly undemocratic. We spent most of our time attending a Communist Youth Camp on the Black Sea near Bourgas, which my mother's friend had arranged for us. This was like a scout camp, with all sorts of outdoor activities. There was some political indoctrination, but in general we enjoyed our time there, competing with the local boys for the attention of the girls. Little did I realise at the time that I would return to the area some 40 years later for my son's wedding to his Bulgaria bride, Maria.

After obtaining my degree, I had to make a big decision about my future. My Russian tutor suggested I could stay on and do a PhD and then become a University lecturer. Tempting as this was, I thought I should not confine my whole life to Academia, although in many ways this is the most suitable occupation for me. I still wanted to do something useful to the community, but had no idea what this could be. So I now did a further two years at Oxford studying for a Diploma in Public and Social Administration (DPSA). I suppose, looking back, this was just an excuse for putting off the time when I would have to earn my own living. Apart from listening to Buddy Holly, the most interesting part of the course was work experience. One task was to design a survey and interview people in Bethnall Green to find out what they did in their leisure time. Surveys are an important part of Social policy, but this one was hardly groundbreaking. We discovered that most people in Bethnall Green watched television after finishing work. My second assignment was to work as an orderly in Tooting Bec Mental Hospital. This was run on the now discontinued lines of a ward system with 20 men in beds who had nothing much to do. I had to shave them, make up the beds (I am now an expert at hospital corners) and generally clear up. Very little effort was put into trying to cure the inmates. Having later visited modern Mental Hospitals, I am happy that this sort of regime has ended, and a more enlightened approach adopted to this distressing illness.

During my time at University two family events stand out. Granny died just after my 21st Birthday. She was the most old-fashioned person I have ever known – Conservative, deeply religious, and totally unaware of how the world was changing. She loved me more than I deserved, largely because I reminded her of her son, Danvers, who died when he was only 19 years old. On one occasion, I posed for a photograph using the same posture of her favourite photograph of him. The two portraits stood together in our drawing room. Also, my middle name is Danvers. She played the piano, like nearly all middle class women of her time. Her favourite tunes were 'Because You're Mine' and 'No Rose in All the World until You Came'. These were sentimental Victorian age songs and I sang them in full voice to her piano accompaniment. It almost brings tears to my old eyes to think about this.

As already mentioned, my sister, Bridget, was doing a secretarial course in Oxford when Robert and I were studying there. One day during the summer vacation, Robert and I were called in by my mother for what sounded like a serious matter. We were shattered when we were told that Bridget was pregnant.

Having been brought up in a very traditional way as far as sex was concerned, this was absolutely shocking to us. We in no way blamed Bridget, and were relieved to hear they planned to get married. It is amazing how much our bourgeois values have changed over the years, although I still think it is wrong to bring a child into the world without a stable background. In Bridget's case, she brought up three impressive sons, Patrick, James and Robert. I stayed with her and her husband when they just had their first two young children while I was working at the mental hospital.

I finally left university at the age of 25. One might have thought that after National Service, University, and working as a courier I would be in a strong position to enter the adult world of work. In fact, it proved more difficult than I thought.

CHAPTER 6

London in the Sixties

I went to live in London to start working for my living in 1962 at the age of 25. This was rather older than most people at the time. I still wanted to do some good in the world, although I now realised this would not be earth-shattering. Having completed my Diploma in Public Service Administration, I went for an interview at the Hospital Administrative Staff College in Bayswater and was accepted for the training course to become a Hospital Administrator. I would have preferred to become a doctor but had studied completely the wrong subjects for that. I hoped that supporting the NHS and helping to improve how it was run was the next best thing. This choice proved a disaster for me, as I am a hopeless administrator. I do not propose to dwell on the work side of this wasted year. The last straw was when I was doing work experience at Worthing Hospital. I had to write a short report for the Hospital Administrator, which was typed up by a secretary. She pointed out, correctly, that I had spelt 'accommodation' wrongly, as I left out the second 'c'. She probably had left school at 16, while I had a degree from Oxford University, but she was right! I also had a problem with the mentor appointed to monitor trainees' progress. He clearly did not think I was up to the job, and even insisted I see a psychiatrist to sort myself out. He was a bit of an amateur psychiatrist and thought my problem was that I was not able to match my father's impressive career. It is true that my father had been an important man and rose to become Governor of Sierra Leone. I was never going to emulate this, but I honestly do not believe this had any effect on my personality. I cannot remember what the psychiatrist advised, but for me it was a complete waste of time. Perhaps if I had taken notice, I would have been more successful, but I doubt it. Anyway, I decided I would not be much use to the NHS and resigned.

21. My Father

Brian Cookson

During the bitterly cold winter of 1963, while I was still in Hospital Administration, my father died. He had spent his working life in the Army in India, and then the Colonial Service in Africa. He was nearly sixty when I was born and suffered poor health partly from having had malaria during his time in Africa. We were never close, but we all admired him greatly. He had retired by the time I was born and seemed to have devoted his life to furthering peace over war. This led him, like many Englishmen, to initially favour rapprochement with Hitler. One of his favourite sayings was 'Jaw, Jaw was better than War, War'. However, he later supported the war effort when the truth about Nazi atrocities came out. I remember him showing me the map of Europe published daily in the Daily Telegraph towards the end of the war. This showed how the Allies lines were advancing to probable victory. I was only seven years old at the time but found it exciting without of course understanding the horror and destruction behind the maps. Then after the war, he and my mother became part of the Peace Movement. They knew the leaders, Bruce Kent and Canon Collins, personally. Again, they wanted peace with the USSR, and in my opinion were reluctant to see the evils of Communism. I had my one and only heated argument with my father over the Soviet invasion of Hungary. I could not believe he would support such a brutal act and the murder of Imry Nagy, the Hungarian Prime Minister. Unfortunately, when one supports a particular point of view strongly, one is easily convinced by that side's propaganda. Up to then I had followed my parents in supporting the Campaign for Nuclear Disarmament (CND). Apart from this sad disagreement, I rated my father highly and was proud of his achievements. His career was recognised by gaining the rank of Captain in the Army and obtaining the accolade of Commander of the Order of St Michael and St George (CMG). I always felt a tingle of pride when addressing him on a letter as Captain Cookson, CMG.

Clearly there was a lot wrong with our colonial history. However, after my father's death, my mother returned to Sierra Leone.

She told me she met people there who remembered my father's Governorship and said how much better life was under the British. Of course, this is not what today's activists, who refuse to see any redeeming features in our colonial history, want to acknowledge. But I am sure he would have been pleased to have heard it. Anyway, I still think of him from time to time, and hope my own children will have similar warm feelings about me when I am gone.

On a more philosophical level, he once quoted me the famous precepts inscribed in the forecourt of the Temple of Apollo at Delphi – 'Know Thyself' and 'Nothing Too Much'. The latter is often rephrased as 'Moderation in all things'. I consider this sound advice and phrases I have also tried to live by. I later visited Delphi with my wife. It is an inspiring sight and reminded me of my father's interest in all things classical.

22. Delphi

On a personal level, the move to London was significant. I had been a country boy at heart. But now I was a man I was about to become a Londoner, which I have been ever since. London in the 'Swinging 60s' was a vibrant place, although the reader will realise by now that I am not really the swinging type. My first lodgings were in the fashionable area of South Kensington. I had a bedsitter which cost £4 per week and was extremely basic. My mother however then very generously bought a mews cottage in Bayswater for myself and my brother, Robert, who was also working in London at the time. The address was 3 Rede Place, which I still use as the basis for some of my many internet passwords. When Robert moved out to go to America, a colleague from the Staff College came to live with me. We shared the same interests and had an equally negative attitude to hospital administration. Nowadays if two people of the same sex live in the same house, it is automatically assumed that they are gay. This never entered my head at the time. We did have two charming neighbours who sang for the D'Oyley Carte Opera Company, and they were definitely gay. Also, there was a pub at the end of the Mews which was very noisy at night and was a popular gay bar. As I mentioned earlier, my friend later lived in a gay relationship. I must admit, this came as a surprise when he told me.

Living in Bayswater was a stark contrast to South Kensington. Even then Bayswater was a very cosmopolitan area, although the Notting Hill Carnival did not start until 1966. London is often called a conglomeration of villages. Each area has its own identity, as I found when moving between these two locations. Little did I realise at this time how important South Kensington was to become for my future life.

Now I was without a job, I had to re-evaluate what to do. After an abortive foray into training in the Berlitz method of teaching English as a foreign language, I went for an interview to teach Russian in a Comprehensive school. It would be humiliating not to have been accepted, since I was a qualified Russian Interpreter and had an Oxford degree in the language. As it turned out, I was humiliated. If administration and teaching were not open to me, I was at a loss as to where I could possibly be useful. Normal professions such as law and medicine were out of the question. They required significant study and I had done enough of that. I then happened to read a book about the brain. This speculated that computers were likely to emulate human intelligence in the future. I found this fascinating. Quite by chance at about the same time, I saw an advertisement in the papers for people of intelligence and initiative to join the Education Department of the world's largest computer company, IBM. I thought I would give it a try, as there was no mention of needing scientific knowledge. I hate interviews, but luckily managed to satisfy the Education Manager that I was capable of teaching. So I embarked on what was to be a 28 year career in computers.

When I joined, computers were in their infancy. Most companies still used the so-called Punch Card machines to do basic tasks such as payroll and accounts. This involved wiring up panels to ensure the holes in the cards produced the right electric impulses to print out the required documents. On our initial IBM training, we were taught how to do this as well as being taught programming languages such as FORTRAN and COBOL as some companies were starting to use real computers.

IBM has been one of the most successful companies the world has ever seen. It was founded by Thomas Watson, who had very pronounced principles on life and business. All employees had to wear dark suits, white shirts and ties. This is largely the reason I still have many white shirts in my wardrobe which I hardly ever use. He also forbade alcohol, initially in both business and private life. Later, when I took customers on sales visits, the culture in the UK was for the IBM team to socialise and buy drinks. On return, expense accounts had to be submitted without any mention of alcohol. This meant various spurious expenses were invented. The British IBM Management turned a blind eye to this procedure.

Once during our initial training, a senior American IBM Manager came over to attend the class presumably to see how the local company was doing, At the end of the class our instructor rather embarrassedly called up a colleague and myself to tell us we had to have a haircut, as the American Manager had complained about the state of the backs of our heads. This reminded me of early days on National Service. Our first reaction was to say, 'Up Yours'. However, this would have brought a possibly lucrative career to a speedy end, so off we went to the nearest barber.

I enjoyed teaching both customers and new IBM recruits. Some of the latter reached much greater heights in the organisation than I ever did. It is still satisfying to know that they learnt something from me, and fun to remember telling some of them off when they made stupid mistakes in class. Highfliers in IBM did not often need to be technically expert, although they had to understand the basics. I soon recognised that there was a pecking order in IBM. Salesmen were the most important class as they brought in the money. I was a Systems Engineer, the name given to technical support staff who were supposed to know how IBM systems could be programmed and used in detail. We were not really engineers in the sense of actually fixing problems with the hardware. This was the job of Customer Engineers.

One of my colleagues in the Education Department was a very clever man, appropriately called Tony Cleaver. IBM was about to launch the world dominating System/360 range of systems. We both spent a whole night in Winchester installing the first ever version in the UK. In those days, system installation took many hours of loading tape reels and sorting out problems. At the time I had no idea of how our careers would develop. We both were rather intellectual types, but Tony went on to become Chief Executive of IBM UK and was knighted by the Queen. My main memory of our long night together in Winchester is that he introduced me to one of my favourite drinks – Gin and Lime.

After five years in the Education Department, I moved to the IBM office in Wigmore Street to work on teleprocessing software development. The system was called 'British Additional Teleprocessing Support', shortened to 'BATS'. This was used by many companies for linking terminals to mainframe System/360 computers. The world's first ATM (automated teller machine) was serviced by this software. It was opened on 27 June 1967, at a branch of Barclays Bank in Enfield, north London, where it can still be seen. Our computer in Wigmore Street was in the basement. I am ashamed to say that we had a view up to the street, and annoyed female colleagues by trying to catch glimpses of girls walking past in '60s miniskirts. Today the computers are long gone, and the building is a Wagamama restaurant.

On a personal level, I took advantage of the many social activities available in London. I had several girlfriends, but no relationship lasted long. Then one day I was invited to a party at the South Kensington flat of Diane, one of the secretaries from the Hospital Administration Staff College. We had remained friends after I left to join IBM.

23. Susan

Across the crowded room I watched fascinated as an attractive girl was holding forth about her career in the RAF. She had not liked the discipline and told the amusing story of how she left after one week. She went to collect her week's pay, but was told wages were payed monthly, so she was given a month's pay. She said she had not done any useful work to deserve this. The cashier joked 'Don't worry, dear, nor have many other people here'. I was smitten and determined I would try and attract her attention. My wooing of Susan was complicated by the fact that I think her friend fancied me. We started going out in foursomes and gradual progress was made. Susan had also been an actress. Never in my wildest dreams did I, a rather reserved bourgeois boy, ever expect to have a relationship with an actress. But although I was out of my depth as far as glamour was concerned, I did have an MG Midget sports car. On one occasion I drove her down to my parent's house in Worthing and that was the beginning of our affair. Our relationship was I believe cemented when Susan's best friend, Sheila, who was married to an architect, invited us both to join them at the annual Architects Ball. We danced till midnight and I was hopelessly in love.

24. Engagement

To cut a long story short, one evening in my home at Rede Place I found myself asking her to marry me. By this time she had shown enough affection for me to hope she would answer 'Yes'. Luckily, she did, and we set a date for the wedding for July 2, 1966. This date is indelibly set in my memory, and not only because I can never forget the year as England won the World Cup shortly after on 30 July. While we were engaged, I met Susan's mother, who was German. She roasted the best leg of pork I have ever had, and seemingly quite liked me. On one occasion I invited Susan and her to Rede Place for tea. I served the milk in its bottle, instead of putting it in a jug. Susan's mother took her daughter to task for this breach of etiquette, and I escaped the blame.

As Susan was a Roman Catholic, I had to agree to get married in St Mary's RC church, near Susan's flat in South Kensington. I also had to be instructed in the faith by the priest and agree that our children be brought up as Catholics. I was too much in love to object even though I had been brought up in the Protestant faith and was now an agnostic.

25. Cutting the Wedding Cake

July 2nd arrived and after the church service, the wedding ceremony was held at the Kensington Gardens Hotel in Knightsbridge. This had only just been built and ours was the first ever wedding booked there. We got a special deal, and the food was excellent. As can be seen from the photograph, Susan looked like a film star. This was one of the happiest days of my life, but I will not go into details, apart from my memory of driving away in the MG with cans attached to the back. I also remember wearing a light grey suit, bought from Whiteleys, the famous store in Queensway. I still have the trousers but only for sentimental reasons as they no longer fit. We stayed the night at Rede Place, before heading off for our honeymoon in the South of France the following morning.

After crossing the Channel, we drove down through Germany by the Rhine. Susan wanted to go this way as she had hitch-hiked there with her friend, Sheila, when they stayed in Youth Hostels. The MG was not ideal for going on a two-week journey through Europe as it had limited luggage space. On one occasion we were stopped by two Gendarmes in France. They said our luggage blocked our view of following traffic, and I thought we were in real trouble. However, Susan flashed her eyes at them, and soon they were helping to rearrange the luggage and wished us a pleasant journey.

26. Casino de Monaco

We stayed at an hotel in Eze-sur-Mer, a small village on the cliffs near Nice. Among other things, we made a trip to Monaco, which is near Menton where my parents first met. I was to return to Monaco some years later at an IBM awards conference. Susan then insisted I limited my gambling stake to £50. I lost it all on Blackjack in five minutes. I know if I am not careful, I could have a gambling problem. I really wanted to bet more but managed to resist the temptation. At the end of the holiday, we drove to Lyon and put the car on the train to avoid another long car journey as we returned to reality.

Susan and I are vastly different characters – she a fiery ex-actress and I a reserved old-fashioned type of Englishman. Opposites do attract, but not always smoothly I must admit. However, I did manage to teach her to drive without causing a divorce. I must admit to an offence when soon after she passed the test, she was caught parking illegally twice in one day. I took the blame for the second offence to avoid her being possibly disqualified. I now know this is a criminal offence. Famously, on one occasion, former Energy Secretary, Chris Huhne and his wife were both sentenced to 8 months in prison after the former convinced the latter to take penalty points from his speeding offence. We were not found out and I have to say I think it disproportionate to receive a jail sentence for this crime.

Susan and I both had jobs we enjoyed and were happy in London. Then, out of the blue, I was asked by an American IBM manager to go to the USA to work on a special project regarding telecommunications for the airline industry. I hardly felt qualified, but we decided to accept. The package was most attractive, with double pay and living expenses covered. We flew to New York and landed at JFK airport. There we had to hire a car to drive to White Plains, just north of New York. We asked for a Compact model, which turned out to be at least twice the size of our MG Midget. It was scary driving on the complex interchanges of the American motorways, especially as I had to drive on the right and had never used an automatic gearbox before. Eventually we arrived in White Plains where we had booked a chalet in the garden of an American University couple. They were polite rather than friendly, as opposed to most Americans we met who were very welcoming. They did tell us where the nearest supermarket was. It was called A&P and located just down the hill from our chalet. We walked there. No-one else would dream of walking to a supermarket in America. It was far larger than any UK supermarket and we soon realised almost everything in America was on a grander scale than in Europe.

My main colleague at work was a German man called Dieter. We became friends with him and his wife, Karen. Susan took up learning German as Karen did not speak English. We went for 'Cookouts' by the River Hudson during the week and camping in the Catskill Mountains in the north of New York State at the weekend.

My mother came over for a visit and accompanied us on one of these outings. Our tent was a cheap basic structure, while most campers had huge motorhomes or sophisticated tents. In the evening we walked up into the forest, without realising that the light faded fast in the Catskills. When we reached the top of a hill, we were in darkness, and not sure of the way back to our tent. I left Susan and my mother there while I ran down to find the way, but twice just returned to where they were. In panic, I tried another path which I thought less likely than the ones I had tried already. Luckily, this led us back safely. Who knows what would have happened if we had had to spend the night in the open, with unknown dangers and cold temperatures? On another night, the message got around the camp that a skunk was on the prowl. The skunk's spray, which has an offensive odour like decaying organic matter, can be aimed accurately at a range of up to 3 metres. We were warned to return to our tent until it went away. Having said this, American camping sites are among the best in the world, and we enjoyed many happy weekends in the mountains.

My brother, Robert, happened to be in Montreal while we were in White Plains, so we drove to Canada to meet up. On our way we took a detour to see Niagara Falls. I was especially enthralled as we approached and saw the Niagara River suddenly disappear ahead of us. We went on a boat at the foot of the Falls and were thoroughly soaked by the spray. Next day we drove on to Montreal, which had played host to Expo 67, considered to be the most successful world's fair in the 20th Century. The modernistic buildings remained until 1984 and contained a fascinating exhibition called Man and His World. I understand this is now all changed, whereas our own Festival of Britain's Royal Festival Hall still stands.

Back in White Plains, two events stand out. The Republicans were about to select their candidate for the upcoming presidential election. Nelson Rockefeller was on the liberal side of the party, challenging the more conservative Nixon. We were in favour of Rockefeller's candidacy, and attended a rally of his supporters. We were astounded at the razzmatazz of the whole occasion and rather put off by the over-the- top adulation of the crowd. In the end, Nixon won, and the rest is history, ending in Watergate.

The other world-shattering event was the Soviet invasion of Czechoslovakia. The invasion successfully stopped Alexander Dubček's Prague Spring liberalisation reforms. Although the majority of the Warsaw Pact supported the invasion along with several other communist parties worldwide, Western nations, along with Albania, Romania, and particularly China condemned the attack, and many other communist parties lost influence. Now of course the Soviet Union and its empire has collapsed. But Stalin is still admired by many Russians and has never received quite the damnation of history that Hitler deservedly got.

After my project in White Plains finished, I was assigned to the IBM laboratories in Raleigh, North Carolina to learn about a new IBM system so I could announce it in the UK. This allowed us to explore the South as far as Florida, which has a vastly different atmosphere from New York. Differences dated back to the American Civil War and we felt there was still some resentment on behalf of some white southerners at their defeat. I had seen 'Gone with the Wind' back in England and found it very moving.

I was naive then about the slavery in the South which is portrayed in the film as benevolent. It is sad that one of the world's greatest films is now seen to be racist as one's sympathies were with Vivien Leigh and her southern friends and relations. Quite rightly, there is no way this film could be made today.

27. Grand Canyon

We also enjoyed a two-week break, which allowed us to fly to Phoenix, Arizona for a tour of the West. We hired a car and stayed in motels as we travelled to the Grand Canyon, Brice Canyon, Zion National Park, Yellowstone and Las Vegas. It is hard to say which of these locations is the most impressive. But I will never forget my first view of the vast gap in the earth's surface ahead of me as we approached the Grand Canyon on foot. We did walk down a third of the way to the bottom to give us an idea of what the early pioneers must have encountered. Later a friend suggested we go on a week's boat ride along the rapids of the Colorado River which snakes its way through the rocks. I regret that we were not brave enough to take up the suggestion.

In Las Vegas, we managed to resist the temptation to gamble except in a small way on slot machines. We did take advantage of a free breakfast in Caesar's Palace, so felt obliged to lose a few dollars there. As we left, we drove to a garage to buy petrol.

There we met an Englishman who served us at the pump. He was clearly well educated but told us he had lost all his money on gambling and now had to remain in Las Vegas until he had paid off his debts.

We had to drive through Death Valley on our final route to San Francisco. Luckily, we had a full tank and plenty of water, as Death Valley is about the hottest and driest place on earth. We made one stop at a watering hole where it was explained that the primitive creatures found there were examples of how life began on our planet. We were relieved when we finally emerged from Death Valley and found a place to stay in Yosemite, which, with its mountains, cascades and trees could not be more different. We ended up in San Francisco and could not believe we had experienced the holiday of a lifetime at IBM's expense. Our one regret was that we were trying for a baby, but so far had no success. We kept trying back in England, and both of us had tests to identify any problems. There were none. Eventually in 1969, Susan became pregnant, and Richard was born 15th February 1970. As with all new parents, this event was to change our lives completely.

I will never forget that night. We were watching 'Funny Girl' with Barbara Streisand in the Notting Hill Odeon Cinema. Suddenly Susan felt contractions coming on, and I rushed her to St Mary's Hospital, Paddington. Several royal babies were born here, including many years later Princes William and Harry, so we were happy this was our local NHS Hospital. I was not allowed in to watch the birth. When I was called in, I was given this little creature to cuddle, which later turned into a 6-foot man - our son.

My IBM office had now moved to Croydon, and Rede Place was not where we wanted to bring up a family. We needed to decide where to move, and that did not prove easy.

CHAPTER 7

Children and Move to Croydon

With little Richard in tow, in early 1970 we explored places like Richmond and Wimbledon to find a house with a garden. Prices were high in these fashionable areas, and transport to my IBM office in Croydon not ideal. We ended up finding a Wates 'Dormy' House with a medium sized garden in Croydon. This cost £12,000 (it is worth about £500,000 today!). It was not far from my office, which was just by East Croydon Station. This meant I could cycle or walk to work, and usually arrived home in time to see Richard to bed. London in the 60's with its social life was replaced by Croydon in the 70's with domestic life at home, and soon national problems such as the three-day week.

28. Richard and Sarah in Rochester Gardens

Not long after our move, Susan again became pregnant, and our daughter, Sarah, was born. I cannot remember why we chose our children's names. I think we just agreed on names we liked. I suggested we avoid any names beginning with 'W', although we quite liked 'William'. This was to avoid the initials 'WC'. As it happens, Richard was the name of Susan's father, while Sarah was the last girlfriend I had before meeting Susan. Sarah was born in our local hospital, which was then called 'The Mayday'. Today it has been renamed 'Croydon University Hospital' but does not seem to have changed much. Like many institutions, it was a mixture of good and not so good. Unfortunately, the Maternity Unit was on the latter end. After the birth, Susan was placed in a small ward and made friends with Jenny, whom we still know. They both said the friendship started as Susan complained vociferously about the conditions. Jenny was not so dramatic a character but was only too pleased to hear Susan having her say. My only significant part was to be sent to M&S to buy Susan a light nightdress. It was unusual for a man to undertake such a task in those days, and I was nervous, being the only male in the lady's department. Seemingly I did alright and both Susan and Jenny were impressed. Susan still wears the nightdress I bought from time to time.

We added a playroom on the ground floor of our house and put up a plunge pool in the summer to improve family entertainment. Susan made friends with several local mothers, one of whom was married to David Prowse, who was famous as the Green Cross Code man, a character used in British road safety advertising aimed at children. Once he came to one of our children's birthday parties, but little did we know at the time we were entertaining the actor who went on to become one of the world's most frightening villains – Darth Vader. A few years later in 1977, the first and in my opinion still the greatest Star Wars film was released. I took Richard and three of his friends to see it at The Dominion Cinema in Tottenham Court Road. We arrived late and walked into the darkened cinema just as a massive starship filled the wide screen to the accompaniment of the booming surround sound. I had never experienced anything like it at the time. We settled into our seats. When the formidable black figure of Darth Vader appeared, I could feel the tension of the boys, who were nearly as scared as I was. I did not realise till later that I had had dinner with him a few years ago. I watched every Star Wars film with Richard until he left home as an adult. Most were great entertainment, but I have not been so impressed with the latest versions. I expect this is my fault and shows how out of tune I am with the modern world.

Life in Croydon was quite traditional for us as a middle-class family. Baby-sitting groups allowed Susan and me to go out on occasion and meet friends. So much happened over the next 30 years up to the end of the century. I will just relate some of my highlights and lowlights, triumphs and disasters.

The first disaster happened when Sarah was three years old. We had not noticed any problem, but my mother saw her less often and one day suggested she was walking awkwardly. We took her to see an orthopaedic surgeon who diagnosed a congenital deformity of her left hip. This required the hip to be broken and reinstated correctly. We were devastated. However, the operation was successful, and Sarah was enclosed in a huge plaster for three months. I had to carry her around as she could not move. We were amazed at how cheerfully she bore the situation.

As it happened, we had booked a holiday in Cornwall soon after her operation. We travelled on the night train from Paddington. One of our fellow passengers was ex-Prime Minister, Harold Wilson. I looked at him and he at me as we boarded the train at the same time. His was such a familiar face I nearly said hello, but thought better of it, so lost my chance to talk to a PM. This was the summer of 1976, one of the hottest on record. We had two weeks of unbroken sunshine, staying in a village near Penzance. Sarah with her plaster on was quite heavy, but I enjoyed her cuddles as I carried her to the beaches. My favourite was Kynance Cove, where a steep path leads down from the cliff head to a beautiful sandy cove surrounded by rocks. We managed most of the famous tourist sites, including Land's End and St Michael's Mount, and filled ourselves with Cornish Pasties and Ice Cream (the real Cornish, not the Walls whale oil and seaweed variety!). I often look back on those two weeks as among the happiest days of my life, thus plucking triumph from disaster. I hope Sarah feels the same despite her operation, although she may hardly remember much as she was just three years old.

29. Fitzjames Avenue swimming pool

In 1977 we moved house to our present home, 26 Fitzjames Avenue. This was larger and had a sizeable garden. It cost us £45,000 at the time. The present value must be over £1 million. We installed a swimming pool, which was enjoyed by the children and their friends and later by our grandchildren. As can be seen in the picture, humans were not the only creatures to enjoy it. Now we are over 80, we found it was too much effort to maintain and it has reverted to lawn.

Over the next 21 years until 1991 I continued to work for IBM. Susan took various editorial jobs. We still use the saucepans she was given when working for 'House and Garden Review'. She later worked at the Citizens Advice Bureau and I was to follow in her footsteps after my retirement.

Family holidays were highlights from everyday life. One of my favourites was our fortnight stay in Cape Sounion in Greece. Our hotel was near the Temple of Poseidon on which Byron had carved his name. This would be unacceptable today even for a famous person, but as Byron fought for Greek independence, it is major tourist attraction. Richard and I took a coach tour of the Peloponnese. We visited the tomb of Agamemnon at Mycenae, and the theatre at Epidaurus. We found out that it is true the acoustics are so good you can hear a pin drop right from the top of the auditorium. For me it was exciting to see the real places where ancient Greek civilisation happened, having studied it as a schoolboy. Homer's Iliad and Odyssey, as well as the plays of Aeschylus, Sophocles, Aristophanes and Euripides were the foundations on which Western literature were built. I can still quote passages I learnt by heart.

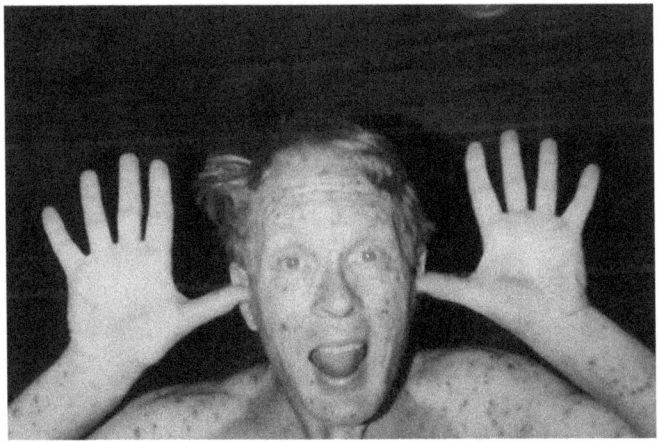

30. Me with chicken pox

In 1982 we flew to Phoenix, Arizona for a two-week tour of the American West. This was almost a repeat of Susan and my earlier exploration of the National Parks, ending up in San Francisco. This time we stayed in Motels, instead of camping. The first few days were not propitious. I felt unusually exhausted after the flight. I bathed in the hotel Jacuzzi to relax soon after arrival. Shortly after this, I came out in hundreds of red spots, which turned out to be chicken pox. We had to make a decision whether to fly straight home or continue while keeping me out of view. We did the latter, which was probably not public spirited, although airlines often do not allow sufferers to fly. I also should have told the hotel to stop people using the Jacuzzi. I never use a public Jacuzzi now! Anyway, as Richard was nearly as tall as me, I hid behind him when eating out. Otherwise I stayed in the hotel room while Susan and the children went sight-seeing. We drove on to Grand Tetons National Park, where we found a doctor as I was not feeling well. His first question was 'when are you leaving the area?' He was pleased to hear we were staying just one day and sent me off with paracetamol.

Luckily I gradually recovered and the children were thrilled by the extraordinary sights, including the General Sherman, a giant sequoia in Sequoia National Park. General Sherman stands 275 feet tall, has a 102-foot circumference, and weighs an incredible 2.7 million lbs. In the end the sheer drama and beauty of the American West outweighed my chicken pox, and we returned to England exhausted, but exhilarated. I visited my local doctor, who told me I was quite lucky to survive, but gave me the all clear.

My career with IBM had its ups and downs, but in general I think I was lucky to have worked for a computer giant while the technology moved on so rapidly. I saw it develop from punched cards in the '60s to PCs in the '90s. Also, the company ethos was to encourage co-operation as well as success. Susan always said work was almost like going to my club. For instance, in the early '80s several of us joined Selsdon Park Hotel golf club. We rose early and played 9 holes before going to the IBM building and having a cooked breakfast before starting work. We had a company on-line diary system where we were supposed to show our daily engagements so that managers and colleagues could book free slots. I was amused on one occasion when our branch manager had rather a lot of golf sessions arranged, and we ribbed him about this. He immediately made his diary private, so only he could see it.

Talking of sport, I later joined Shirley Park Golf Club, where I still play. I managed to achieve an 11 Handicap at one time, and my name can be seen on some of the competition boards in the club bar. One of my partners, Davis Horne, and I won the Summer 4 Ball in 1986.

31. Shirley Park Golf Club 3rd Tee

On one frightening occasion we were about to drive off at the third tee, when he felt faint and said he thought he had a heart attack. We had no mobile phones then. I had to run to the club house to phone for an ambulance. I told them where the third tee was and rushed back to find David sitting slumped on a bench by the tee. No-one came for a quarter of an hour, so I dashed back to the club house to find the ambulance had arrived but had not listened to my request to go to the third tee. I restrained my frustration and we drove to pick David up and take him to the hospital. He recovered, but sadly later died of another heart attack. Unfortunately, on a later occasion, another sporting friend, Les Novell, was drinking with me and two other tennis players in the garden of The Crown Public House. Suddenly he slumped backwards, and I managed to grab him to stop him falling. This time the ambulance arrived promptly, and I went with him to the hospital. He never fully recovered and died in a nursing home.

I myself have had too many hospital encounters. I will just relate one near death experience. I had just returned from an IBM project in America and was somewhat jet-lagged. Next day I had to meet a customer in Maidenhead. In those days it was obligatory to have a drink in a pub if the customer wanted. I drank a pint of London Pride, which was within the limits for driving, and then drove home on the M4. I felt relaxed and decided I should keep to the 70mph speed limit. Probably if I had been driving faster, I would have had to concentrate more, and I would not have ended up in the central reservation with my windscreen broken. I must have lost consciousness as I remember nothing until I saw a policeman and an ambulance. The policeman accompanied me to the hospital and clearly wanted to interview me about the accident. The doctor said I was in no fit state to be interviewed, so the policeman left. The hospital informed My IBM manager about what had happened, and it was he who told my wife. She must have had quite a shock. When she visited me in hospital next day, I was less dazed, and soon returned home. Now the policeman did come to see me, but by now I realised what could happen if I admitted I had probably fallen asleep at the wheel. There are a wide range of penalties, from fines and driving bans to imprisonment. However, the prosecution has to prove you fell asleep, so I simply said I could not remember anything. After three visits, the policeman gave up, and I was not charged.

I did get what was for me a worse punishment. At one time I had reached the men's singles finals of Shirley Park Tennis Club, and had played against former England Davis Cup representative, Geoff Paish. But after my shoulder had been severely injured in the accident, I could never play tennis as well. This probably led to my recent even worse health problem with my neck, resulting in a Cervical Laminectomy. This involved removing five bones from my cervix to allow the spinal cord to function. This has left me with permanent pins and needles in my left arm and reduced physical strength. At least I recovered well enough to play tennis and golf with my friends, but while I used to be about the best in both groups, I am now the worst - 'O Tempora O Mores' as Cicero said in disgust at the state the Roman world had come to. I should not really complain as it was largely my own fault.

32. Letter from the General

To my own surprise, I followed Susan's steps into amateur dramatics with a company run by a local Estate Agent. Susan had starred in several plays as she had been a professional actress. The company was short of men, so I put in two appearances. First as a 25-year-old bridegroom – I was 40 years old at the time, and then in 'Letter from the General'.

At IBM I constantly had to learn new systems. IBM is said to stand for 'I've been moved'. I will concentrate on a few of my most memorable experiences. My most successful marketing coup started unpropitiously. Commercial Union were looking to install a computer system in each of their branch offices, all linked to their mainframe IBM System/360 in Whyteleafe, near Croydon. I was leading the technical team trying to convince them to use a new IBM System called 1800. I knew a customer in Peterborough had installed an 1800, so persuaded the Commercial Union decision maker, Tony Turner, to go with me to find out how effectively it worked. Turner was known as a highly intelligent man, but not too favourable to IBM. I had crossed his path before when we lost out to a competitor for data base software. Anyway, we agreed to meet at King's Cross one morning to catch the 8.30 train to Peterborough. He was bringing two of his computer experts with him. When I arrived at King's Cross, I saw the Peterborough train was about to leave. I made a spur of the moment decision to jump on, only to find out I had caught the 8.15 train, and so would not meet the Commercial Union group as agreed. I was desperate and sure I had completely messed up our marketing campaign. I got off the train at the next stop, St Albans, and phoned King's Cross Station asking them to call for Tony Turner. There were no mobile phones then. When Turner came to the phone, he said he was just about to catch the next train when I called him to the phone, so now he had missed it. I expected him to cancel the trip, but in fact he agreed to catch the next train and join me at St Albans. When I finally met the group, they were highly amused, and the session ended with a successful visit to the customer. As a result, Commercial Union did install many 1800 systems, and Turner delighted in telling the story of my misadventure whenever we met. We came to quite like each other, and on a later occasion I accompanied him to the USA to learn how some American companies, such as Boeing, were using the system. At the end of the trip, Tony wanted to go skiing. It was mid-June, but there was still just enough snow on the mountains at Denver. We were among the last people to ski that year, and it was the last time I myself had the pleasure of skiing. This fact was sad for me, as we had so many family holidays in The Alps, starting with the Sedrun venture when I first fell in love as already mentioned. There can be no more exhilarating feeling than standing on the top of a snow-covered mountain with azure blue skies and bright sunshine. The anticipation of danger as one looks down at a black piste adds to the thrill.

One skiing holiday was almost a disaster. I took Richard and Sarah to Mayrhofen in Austria when they were quite small. Susan does not like skiing so stayed at home. I left them at the beginner's ski school while I skied on my own. When I returned at lunchtime, I found that Sarah had bumped heavily into a post and had been taken to hospital with broken ribs. She was remarkably cheerful, but I blamed myself for leaving her. I had to decide whether to tell Susan, and decided it was better not to worry her. When we returned to Gatwick, we were driven in a trolley as Sarah could not walk. Susan was horrified to see what had happened, and I was in the doghouse for some time. 'Mea culpa' to some extent I suppose.

To return to IBM, one of my most fascinating projects involved a week in Moscow. This was during the time when there was a partial thaw in relations between the USSR and The West after Brezhnev had met Nixon. The Russians were developing a massive complex in the Urals to mine iron ore, make steel and end with finished products such as Lorries. Their computers were well behind the Americans and they wanted to buy an IBM mainframe to control the process. IBM was not allowed to sell their latest machines as it was feared the Russians would learn too much and be able to build their own advanced systems. However, an IBM team had done an initial review in Moscow, and now had been asked to present their proposal in detail. The IBM experts did not speak Russian and had to rely on a Soviet interpreter. They wanted someone on their team who understood what was being interpreted as they did not trust the other side. I was asked to go with the team for the second visit purely in my capacity as a Russian speaker. As it happened, I did know something about the technical details of the proposal.

I was warned that, on the first visit, members of the team had been approached by young women for sex. This was presumably an attempt at blackmail. As it happened, no woman tried it on with me, or as far as I know with fellow members of the team. The discussions lasted a week, and I came to despise the leading American presenter, who started off by claiming that this would be a partnership like a marriage. I sensed the Russian interpreter's embarrassment at having to translate this. The American and I nearly came to blows when we had both drunk too much vodka on the last night. He was dismissive of the Russian bass singer who sang some of my favourite Russian songs, while I said how great it was to hear his rich rendition of folk music. Luckily, we left Moscow the next day. Eventually the Kama River project developed into a massive production site, and many western companies won contracts in the area of engineering and steel making, all controlled by our mainframe.

On a personal level, we found our children turning into adolescents. As most parents probably find, this is a difficult time. Richard became friends with a charismatic boy who was on the verge of being a criminal. I did benefit as one day he gave me a whole bag of golf balls, which presumably he had originally intended to sell, but seemingly wanted to curry favour with me as his friend's father. Luckily, I do not think Richard ever did anything really bad and grew out of this particular relationship.

33. Me in the Wooden Horse at Troy

Family holidays had always been an important part of our lives, but in 1988 Susan and I risked having our first holiday abroad without the children. We travelled to Turkey and spent two weeks there, starting in Istanbul and touring to Antalya on the south coast via Troy, Ephesus and Pammukale. It was exciting to see so many of the historic sites I had read about, and to end up relaxing in a luxury hotel near a sandy beach. We were especially impressed by our visit to Hagia Sophia in Istanbul. It had been built in the 6th Century as a Byzantine Cathedral but became a Mosque when the Moslems conquered Constantinople in 1453. Ataturk made this into a museum as part of his secularisation of Turkey after the First World War. We saw both Christian icons and Moslem calligraphy on the walls of the building. The awe-inspiring beauty of the vast interior with emblems of both religions side by side was a moving expression of mutual respect. Sadly, the present President of Turkey, Erdogan, seems to have turned from being a relatively liberal ruler into an ardent Islamist and has changed the building back into a Mosque. I only hope the spirit of Ataturk will rise again after Erdogan departs.

34. Richard's Doctorate at York University

Meanwhile, Richard and Sarah were growing from teenagers to adulthood, with a variety of girlfriends and boyfriends, both suitable and unsuitable. Luckily, no serious damage was done, and both went on to University. Richard went to York to get a degree in Philosophy, Politics and Economics, and now is a Professor of Health Economics at York University.

35. Sarah's Graduation at Leeds University

Sarah got her degree in English and Philosophy, after which she took a Law degree. Now she works as a Lawyer in the Home Office, managing a team of lawyers who worked on many projects, including locking down the country when COVID-19 hit in Spring 2020. We are immensely proud of our children's achievements. Could we possibly take some credit? Sarah got married in the 21st Century, which is beyond the scope of my 20th Century story. She has two children, Lyra and Lani. I will relate how Richard got married in the next chapter.

CHAPTER 8

Retirement and Afterlife

36. Mummy at an International Peace Conference

My mother died in 1991, at the age of 89. She had a profound influence on my upbringing, which helped shape my character as a typically inhibited middle class Englishman, born in the 1930s, with a drive to learn and pursue what I considered useful activities. I like to think it also imbued me with a social conscience and a hatred of injustice. She herself was an imposing character. I already mentioned her involvement in the Peace Movement. After her death, members of the local CND held a ceremony in the garden of her house to plant a tree in honour of her contribution to the cause. The speeches showed how much everyone admired her. I did not always agree with her, but I know she worked tirelessly for what she believed in. Although not actually a politician she worked in the political arena. If all politicians were as honest and diligent as her, the world would be a better place.

In 1991, IBM was looking to reduce staff numbers and I was offered a great retirement package. After much reflection I decided to take it. Inflation had come right down from the dizzy heights of the 1980s, so we would be comfortably off even if I did not get another job. As you will have gathered, I am too driven a character to just enjoy myself, so I made a list of activities to keep me out of mischief. Before I could really try out any of these, I was offered a part time job by a former colleague from IBM who had become managing director of a firm which developed computer based insurance applications. I was put in charge of the technical aspects of their products for the UK. The developers were in Austin Texas, so I had several trips there. They had very advanced ideas, but unfortunately the main PC based product did not perform well. I eventually took a customer to Austin to evaluate it. He was not impressed. I could not disagree with him, and so fell out with the developers. As a result I left the company. So ended my career in computers. The future was all about Personal Computers, Internet and smartphones. Despite 30 years in the industry, and surviving massive changes, I struggle with keeping up with new technology today.

In the 1990s, our children were growing from teenagers to adulthood. First University, and then careers in Academia and the Law as I already mentioned. This meant Susan and I could make our own lives more or less as before having children, although we were rather older. Both of us had new ventures, including working at the Citizens Advice Bureau (CAB in those days).

Debt, divorce, benefits and neighbour disputes were among the most common problems we encountered at the CAB. As an old fashioned middle class Englishman I did find some of the training overly Politically Correct. One of the men on my course was from the north, and referred to our female teacher as 'love' on one occasion. She tore into him for being a male chauvinist. He just said that was how people addressed each other in his community. I cannot help feeling people are too easily offended in the modern world. I was taught to take the rough with the smooth, but I suppose I am a privileged white Anglo-Saxon so cannot understand how other sexes, classes and races feel. On a more amusing level, I loved some of the training questions we had to answer. My favourite was how to handle a situation when the client started to cry. There were two main approaches and we had to select the better:

1. Pull yourself together, woman, crying won't help solve the problem
2. It's quite alright to cry – I will go and get you a cup of tea and bring back some helpful information from our system.

Even I got this right!

I worked at the CAB two days a week for eight years until 2001. I decided to give it up then, partly because the systems were becoming very bureaucratic. Instead of spending most of our time trying to help clients, we had to make sure we wrote very thorough notes which would later be inspected by central office. The balance between helping clients and satisfying CAB policy makers had changed so much that we could only handle about four clients a day instead of eight. I did not want to spend my time pandering to the bureaucrats rather than helping people. Having said that, I did find my time at the CAB rewarding. A huge amount of information was available, allowing us to really help people with such a variety of problems. Most clients expressed their gratitude. There are few better feelings than when one has been helpful to another human being, especially when they are in trouble. We also learnt so much about how the nation works, so were better able to handle any of our own problems.

The other reason I decided to leave was that I had started a new part time career. As I mentioned, on retirement from IBM I had made a list of possible activities to pursue. One had been to bring my golf handicap down to single figures. I did get down to an 11 handicap, but failed to achieve single figures. So I decided to just play golf for pleasure and concentrate on my idea of training to become a London Tourist Board Blue Badge Guide (BBG).

I had to undergo an interview and written test to even get on the course. We were shown some previous tests so I managed to swat up on the sort of subjects involved. The questions ranged from the easy, such as 'How many wives did Henry VIII have?' to trickier, such as 'Where in London is Dickens's House?' The answers are 'Six' and 'Doughty Street'. I am quite good at swatting, so passed this test. The interview was more scary. I think I managed to pass largely because I had been a Russian Interpreter and they wanted foreign language speakers. Fortunately, no one at the interview spoke Russian, so they did not realise my Russian was rather rusty. I later failed the Russian Language Tourist Board oral exam and was not allowed to guide in Russian! The BBG course lasted two years, with sessions in the evenings and weekends to allow people with jobs to participate. We had to learn detailed background information on topics such as history, politics, education, agriculture, art and architecture. In addition we had lectures on major sites such as Tower of London and Westminster Abbey. At weekends we visited places such as Bath, Oxford and Canterbury, where we would later take parties of tourists by coach. The weirdest exercise was learning how to run a coach tour of London. 15 of us would ride in a mini-bus, and take it in turns to do the commentary on what we saw. The tricky part was that the guide had to sit looking backward at the others, so as to have eye contact. This meant that we had to know exactly what sites were coming up, without being able to see them. Also, as we were sitting backwards, we had to point out a building which we were approaching on the left with our right hand, and vice versa.

37. Blue Badge Guide card

The final exam was stressful. There were written tests which were much harder than the one we did before the course. We also had to guide in major London attractions, and do the commentaries in the mini-bus. I thought I might have failed the latter as my mini-bus got stuck in traffic in Victoria Street, just before we reached Parliament Square. I knew that silence was not an option. As a General Election was about to come up, I managed to waffle on about politics and the history of Parliament. Anyway, I was overjoyed when the results came out and I became a qualified BBG. This was in 1997. As can be seen from my business card, I later published two books on London.

Rather confusingly, the orange badge for disabled people was soon replaced by the blue disabled badge. Today I sometimes have phone calls from people enquiring about the Blue Badge scheme, as that is much better known than the Blue Badge Guide qualification. One benefit is that I manage to avoid queues for security at the British Museum by informing the security attendant that I am a Blue Badge Guide. Probably they think I am disabled as I am so old.

Initially I worked mainly on coaches, which provide the staple income for many BBGs. They are run by major companies such as Evan Evans and Golden Tours. The guide is expected to keep up a commentary for most of the way to places like Bath, Stonehenge or Oxford, and then give guided walking tours around the destination. For the coach commentaries, I found myself immersed in studying all aspects of the English countryside, with a special emphasis on different types of crops. I rather doubt if most of the tourists were particularly interested in this, but I was only doing what we were taught. I much preferred showing people the amazing architecture and talking about the history of some of Britain's most beautiful towns. As the market was intended mainly for foreign tourists, especially Americans, tours included as many destinations as possible. I remember Bath being especially arduous, as we visited Stonehenge and Salisbury on the way. By the time I had done the guided tour of Bath itself, including the Roman Baths, everyone must have been exhausted. This meant I could let them sleep on the return journey to London. We normally only got back at about 8pm, having started off at 9am.

After the excitement of meeting a new challenge, I found the experience of coach tours was too stressful, even if financially rewarding. As I was not so interested in the money as enjoying a new venture, I decided to give up the coach tours and try to enter the world of walking tours. I joined a small London walking tours enterprise called 'Stepping Out'. I attended some tours given by them, so that I could fill in when no one else was available. I also did my own research to develop a new walk for them, which I entitled 'Rebels, Radicals and Rough Justice'. The walk starts at Farringdon which was the terminus of the first Underground Line in the world. The title – Rebels, Radicals and Rough Justice- characterises the rest of the route. The walk follows the footsteps of Wat Tyler, leader of the Peasant's Revolt of 1381, and William Wallace, Scottish patriot. Both met violent deaths in Smithfield, where cattle were also slaughtered until 1855. On the route we meet Lenin who lived here before he overthrew the Russian Tsar, as well as seeing three ancient monasteries and London's oldest hospital. It ends by the Old Bailey, the Central Criminal Court. This was built on the site of Newgate prison, where many famous inmates were incarcerated before being publicly executed until the 19th Century.

38. William Wallace Memorial, Smithfield

Stepping Out advertised tours in several parts of London. We guides turned up at Tube Stations hoping a reasonable number of people would turn up. Unfortunately, often only a few came, and occasionally no one at all. I really enjoyed this type of guiding but was not happy with waiting for clients to turn up and sometimes going back home without doing a tour.

I found out about another venture, called 'Town and Around'. This was run by an elderly man who used to do walking tours himself, but now employed guides to do the tours he advertised on a mailing list. The profits were shared. The mailing list was the key to his success as he had built up a clientele who were known to be interested in attending tours. Normally between 20 and 40 people came. This was much more satisfying than the Stepping Out experience. I spent much time inventing new walking tours, as well as visits to galleries and other places of interest. However, after a couple of years, the owner died. Fortunately I had got to know several of the regular attendees, so was able to build up my own mailing list. I formed a new venture, which I called 'London Explorers'. I built my own website and advertised it on the internet. I then got a call from someone who objected that I was using the name of his own site. I do not know if this was illegal, but decided not to have a quarrel. I renamed my venture 'Discovering London' and I ran tours under this name until the Coronavirus struck in 2020.

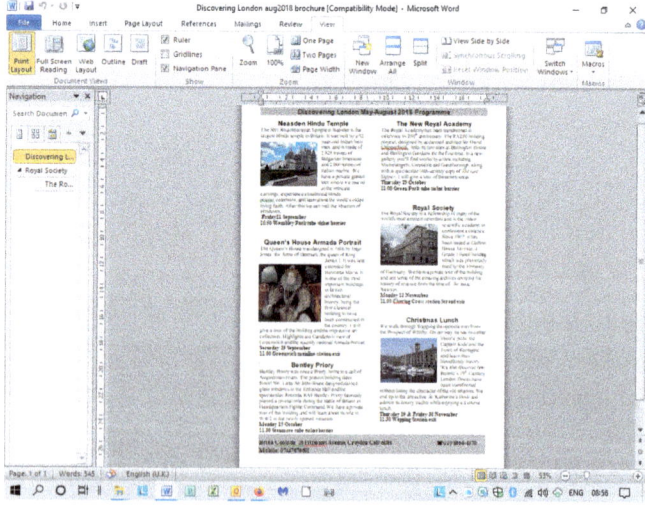

39. Discovering London Programme

I also got a part time job at the City Literary Institute (City Lit), running London Walks courses. My first 8 week course was called 'Literary London'. This covered areas mainly in central London connected with Shakespeare, Dickens (2 walks), Oscar Wilde, the Bloomsbury Group, as well as a variety of authors and playwrights in Clerkenwell and around Fleet Street. I did eight sessions each term, adding up to 24 per year. After working there for three years I had built up a catalogue of 72 walking or museum and gallery tours in all parts of London. London may not be as beautiful as perhaps Paris or Rome. But no other city in the world has the excitement and variety of localities and history found here. What also excites me as a tour guide is London's idiosyncrasy. For example, walking past the modernistic Lloyds Building, by Richard Rogers, one suddenly finds oneself in the Victorian gothic Leadenhall market; also the medieval St Helen's Church stands almost hidden next to the 21st Century 62-storey building at 22 Bishopsgate. Above all I love the variety of its river bridges, from the shimmering beauty of Albert Bridge and the nineteenth century Gothic extravaganza of Tower Bridge to the streamlined elegance of the twenty-first century Millennium Bridge. This inspired me later to write my book on London's bridges, 'Crossing the River', published by Random House.

I was forcibly retired from the City Lit at the age of 65, much to my annoyance. This was before it was made illegal to dismiss people on the basis of age. Fortunately, a colleague had been running similar courses for Sutton College of Learning for Adults (SCOLA). He decided to give up, and handed the work over to me. I have been running these courses now for over 20 years, both at City Lit and SCOLA. I find luck and chance play a great part in one's life. This time they were on my side.

40. Richard and Maria's Wedding with Parents

After a number of girlfriends, our son Richard met Maria when they were both at York University. She was the daughter of Dora, who had been a high ranking Communist in Bulgaria before Communism collapsed in Eastern Europe. They decided to get married in a church just outside York, and the wedding reception was held at York Racecourse. After the wedding, they went to Bulgaria to celebrate their marriage in a second ceremony. Susan and I travelled to Bourgas and met Maria's many relatives during a week's stay. This was wonderful but rather strenuous, as we usually had more than one visit arranged every day. The Bulgarians were very hospitable, so we felt we had to eat and drink a lot on each occasion.

41. My Speech at the Bulgarian Wedding Ceremony

Finally, we attended the ceremony, and I was asked to make a speech in Russian. By the time my turn came, I was fairly drunk and nearly fell over on climbing on to the stage. Anyway, possibly as a result of the Bulgarian rakia (the local firewater), I entered into the spirit of the Russian language, and returned to my seat in somewhat of a daze. Afterwards, several people said they could not believe an Englishman could speak Russian so well. This was very flattering coming from people who had been brought up under Communism to learn Russian. I do not know what their feelings were about the fact I had learnt the language during National Service. This was in the Cold War when Bulgaria was on the opposite side. Richard and Maria eventually settled in Durham, where they had two children, Laura and Harry, and pursued careers in academia.

42. Sarah outside 10 Downing Street

Brian Cookson

Our daughter, Sarah, joined the Home Office in the legal department, where she often meets Ministers giving advice on matters of law. She married Tim early in the next century and lives in St Leonards-on-Sea with her two children, Lyra and Lani.

Now Susan and I were on our own, we became more adventurous in our holidays. I feel I could write another book about our travels but will confine myself here to two of our most distant and exotic tours.

In 1990 we flew to China. We spent two weeks in the Republic of China, followed by 10 days in Hong Kong and Thailand. China had emerged from the harsh cruelties of Chairman Mao's rule, but was still a Totalitarian Communist regime. The Tiananmen Square Massacre had taken place the year before our visit. A mass student-led demonstration against corruption and the lack of democracy was brutally suppressed. Troops armed with assault rifles and accompanied by tanks fired at demonstrators and those trying to block the military's advance into Tiananmen Square. Estimates of the death toll vary from several hundred to several thousand. By the time we arrived, the nation had been pacified. Our tour was organised by the Communist authorities to show how well they governed the country.

43. China Socialism Slogan

We had previously done a tour of East Germany when it was under Communist rule. Again the tour implied that East Germans lived in a Worker's Paradise. The propaganda was most convincing. However, not long after, the Wall was pulled down, and the truth emerged. In China, visits were arranged to Collective Farms, factories and schools. The people seemed content, although Health and Safety was far below Western standards in factories. Beneath the surface we were not so sure that all was well. Certainly, the locals I talked to on the sea front in Shanghai mainly wanted to know about life in England, as they did not believe in China's Government propaganda.

44. Shanghai Locals

The roads were filled with bicycles. We wondered what would happen if people started to own cars as there was no room for more traffic. There seemed to be a hierarchy for motorised vehicles. Official cars had precedence through the traffic, followed by tourist coaches like ours. Ordinary car owners came last. But in general it did seem that China was going through a period of dramatic change. We could not possibly have imagined how the country would look like 30 years later. In 2020, China rivals America in most respects. We would not recognise the modern megacities which have replaced the old fashioned low-rise urban landscape of 1990. I must say that the propaganda visits were very interesting, even if they did not tell the whole story.

45. Susan at Xian with Terracotta Warrior

The highlights of our tour were of course the amazing historic sites, such as the Great Wall, the Forbidden City and Xiang. At Xiang we looked down at the huge pit where hundreds of Terracotta Warriors were lined up. We were told not to take photographs, but one person thought they could take a photo surreptitiously. The Chinese attendants immediately arrested him. I think he just had to hand over his camera, but I would rather not tangle with the Chinese authorities. We were more careful, and I took a picture of Susan with a warrior placed in the nearby museum. We also ordered a half-sized terracotta Warrior to be shipped to England. This now stands in the hall of our house. It did arrive in two pieces as terracotta is friable. I managed to stick it together with glue so that he looks fine.

For us Westerners, the whole experience of China was mind-blowing. The main downside was the food. We had visited a market where we saw live snakes squirming in a large bowl, until someone ordered one. Then the seller picked out a snake and skinned it alive. In the hotels, our food was served on a Lazy Susan turntable, with no menu to indicate what we were actually eating. Having been to the live food market, this was disconcerting.

After two weeks of eating Chinese food, we were relieved to go on to Hong Kong where we eagerly sampled a Macdonald's burger. Hong Kong was still under British rule, although much of the dynamism came from the Chinese. It was as business-like and commercialised as any modern city, with iconic skyscrapers such as Norman Foster's HSBC Headquarters building. The British Lease was to run out in 1997, so we wondered what would happen when the Chinese took over. In fact, Hong Kong was not democratic under British rule. However the impression is that towards the end the Chinese inhabitants were given much more say in how the place was governed. Today, many local Chinese are protesting against China's attempts to integrate Hong Kong into the mainland Communist system.

After six days in Hong Kong, we flew to Bangkok in Thailand. The traffic there was even worse than in Shanghai, with a greater proportion of cars and tuk-tuks. The Grand Palace is as amazing as anything we had seen in China. For me the highlight was having a bespoke Mohair suit made and fitted in one day for less than £50. I still wear this after 30 years.

We had made friends with another couple and agreed to go with them to Australia the following year. In Sydney we especially admired two contrasting structures. The Sydney Harbour Bridge was designed and built in 1932 by British firm Dorman Long of Middlesbrough (who based the design on their Tyne Bridge in Newcastle upon Tyne). The bridge is nicknamed "The Coathanger" because of its arch-based design. The Sydney Opera House was designed in a dramatic modern fashion by Danish architect Jørn Utzon. It was opened in 1973 and is one of the 20th century's most famous and distinctive buildings. It is now a UNESCO World Heritage Site.

46. Sydney Opera House

After Sydney, we went to Palm Cove. I ventured to scuba dive down into the Great Barrier Reef. Experienced instructors showed us what to do and accompanied us on the dive. I was told afterwards that one should have a certificate of competence to do this, although it is not actually illegal. In fact I felt scared, but excited and saw the most amazing coloured coral and exotic fish close up. One other diver was not so lucky. The instructor noticed he had trouble breathing on the way down. He was brought up safely to the surface but missed the dive and did not get his money back.

47. Susan and Me at Uluru

Our next venture was to the Red Centre. After the excitement of scuba diving, I had not expected to have an even more thrilling experience. But when I saw Uluru and we were told we could climb it at dawn, I decided to have a go. I struggled to keep my footing on the steep smooth surface at the bottom and kept on slipping back. Susan watched my desperate efforts for a while before the coach took the non-climbers back to the hotel. She told me afterwards she had been worried she might not see me again. Eventually I reached a more level stretch and looking down from the summit I felt as if I was on top of the world. I had not thought about this at the time, but Uluru is sacred to the Indigenous Peoples. Climbing Uluru is now forbidden.

48. Christchurch Cathedral

On a later visit to Australasia, we were lucky to visit New Zealand before the earthquake devastated Christchurch. Susan took the picture above showing the fine Gothic style building, completed in 1904. The picture below shows the destruction following the earthquake. The cathedral has not been rebuilt yet, but I understand there is now a plan to do so.

49. Christchurch Cathedral after the Earthquake

While in Christchurch we learnt a surprising fact. Christchurch seemed to be like England used to be about 50 years ago, and much more traditional. But we saw a memorial to New Zealand Suffragettes, and a plaque which informed us that women won the right to vote as early as 1893. This was 25 years before British women were allowed to vote.

50. New Zealand Suffragette Memorial

We later were entertained by Maori dancers and discovered how well they are integrated into New Zealand Society. We were impressed by the beauty of the often dramatic landscape of New Zealand, as well as its culture. If I was asked to choose another country apart from England as my home, I think it would be New Zealand.

51. 30th Wedding Anniversary

Back home we celebrated our 30th Wedding Anniversary in our garden at 26 Fitzjames Avenue, Croydon. It was a wonderful feeling to be surrounded by so many relatives and friends, including my elder half-sister, Anne. She was an impressive lady, and became Chair of the Women's Institute in Britain. None of us other siblings achieved such high status, although my brother, Robert, had a distinguished career running Economics courses for the Open University. My sister, Bridget, was a Social Worker for many years, and now does an amazing amount of voluntary work in schools and charity shops. Our son and daughter made lovely speeches about us. I believe some guests took a plunge in the swimming pool, but I was far too drunk to risk this. The sun shone for our garden party and on our marriage.

Looking back on our life together, there is of course no doubt that Susan has been the most important person in my life. I cannot pretend our marriage has been entirely calm. Susan has a fiery personality, whereas I am a much colder type. But our quarrels do not last long. Susan has helped bring me out of my shell and now I meet the world with much more confidence than I did as a shy young man. She is also the most caring person I know, with a hatred of all kinds of injustice. Luckily we have many shared interests and values, including travel, art and playing bridge. At one time she decided she preferred to play with another man as a partner. His name happened to be James Bond. I was a bit jealous, but do not believe anything happened!

Susan has had a variety of interesting jobs. These included editorial positions, a post in the Central Office of Information, and voluntary work in the Citizen's Advice Bureau, as well as being an official guide in Tate Britain, Tate Modern and the Dulwich Art Gallery. Her love of art partly inspired me to qualify as a guide myself, and we have on occasion taken groups around Tate Britain and the British Museum together. However, I fear I have not kept up with her in her appreciation of Modern Art.

Above all, I am so grateful that she devoted her life for a time to bring up our children, which allowed me to pursue my career with IBM. Both Richard and Sarah have told me what a wonderful mother she was – and still is – taking them to play groups, helping with homework, and dealing with friendship issues. I like to think I did my best to help, but Susan deserves most of the credit for bringing up two such impressive personalities.

On a lighter note, we share a love of chocolate and ice cream. In addition, I have to hide the bottle of Bailey's or it soon gets emptied. As far as cooking is concerned, her chocolate cake and steak and kidney pudding are legendary.

One amazing benefit to me in writing this book was Susan's interest in photography. We now have a pictorial record of our lives dating back to the birth of our son in 1970, and many of the pictures here are from Susan's many books of photographs. So for so many reasons I have to thank her for agreeing to be my life partner and mother to our children.

52. Cooksons at Christmas

Other family gatherings included dining on the top storey of the Hilton Hotel, Park Lane. In the picture are Robert and Bridget in the front, with Robert's wife, Ana and his children, Edward and William, then Richard and Sarah, and me in the background.

Life in Croydon without children was a new challenge. Our house and garden are really much too big for two aging people. But the children both liked visiting especially in summer where they enjoyed swimming in our outdoor pool. Later they came with their own children and we decided to stay put. Now it is too late to face up to moving, although we did recently look at a retirement home. Having been used to living in a large house, we did not feel happy with the idea of being confined to a two bedroom apartment, even though there were communal areas. Also it seems a very expensive way to solve the problems of maintaining a large property.

53. Big Ben at Midnight

My story ends with the passing of the millennium. Susan's great friend, Bobby, had contacts with JP Morgan, and we spent the evening of 31 December 1999 on their boat. This was moored just opposite the Houses of Parliament. We drank a toast to the familiar old century as Big Ben struck 12 times to welcome in the new one. After a fireworks display, the boat sailed down to Greenwich. Here a laser beam showed the line of the meridian, which is symbolic as it was from this exact spot that the new millennium really began. All other countries could only measure their time from here, although they probably did not concern themselves with this fact.

I have no idea how we got home that morning, but I do remember feeling nostalgia for my birth century and wondering what the future held for us in the new millennium.

Brian Cookson

Epilogue

Susan and I are still alive in 2020 in the midst of the Coronavirus pandemic. This gave me the chance to write of my experiences in the last century, and reflect back on what I have learnt. Although I have much enjoyed my second career as a London Blue Badge Guide, I decided not to cover the 21st Century in this book. I still think of myself as a 20th Century character, somewhat out of place in the modern world. I will end with a few comments on what I have found to be important issues. I am sure I shall appear as a grumpy old man, but here goes.

There have been many improvements in society since I was born. Women and ethnic minorities play a bigger part than they used to. In general, Britain is a much fairer place to live in. I agree there is further to go, and we should constantly be seeking to reform where necessary. I understand that reforming groups feel the need to be strident to achieve their objectives, but I cannot accept that they should intentionally disrupt ordinary people's lives in our democratic society. Also many campaigning groups seem to think Britain is an awful country. Actually, in my opinion, we are very lucky to live here rather than under so many of the oppressive regimes in other parts of the world. I would ask why so many migrants want to come to Britain if our society is as bad as some people make out.

I was brought up as a Christian, but lost my faith in my 20s. I consider myself an agnostic, because atheist implies I know what nobody can possible know, as the dead cannot tell us the truth. Considering the huge number of religions and sects within religions, I find it extremely unlikely that just one of them is right. However, I respect each person's right to believe, and many believers contribute in a positive way. Unfortunately this is not always the case. In the past, Catholics and Protestants have killed each other for their beliefs. Today the problem is mainly Islamic Extremism, where fanatics are even prepared to kill themselves in order to damage society. I believe fanaticism in all its forms is one of the greatest dangers we face. It breeds a bigoted self-righteousness where other people's opinions are not respected. I myself plead guilty to this sort of feeling when I was on the Aldermaston March together with so many people who believed the same thing. By all means we should struggle for what we believe is right, but not at the expense of common humanity.

53. Chinese Schoolchildren

I recently saw Michael Palin's travelogue '80 Days around the World'. He concluded that most people he met in all the countries he visited wanted to get on with their lives and be friendly to others, regardless of race, sex or religion. I have found this too, and attach my favourite photograph from our visit to China. Here I met a group of schoolchildren, being taken on an outing by their teacher. He can be seen smiling as I taught them how to do an exploit I learnt as a child called 'Here's the church, and here's the steeple. Open the doors, and there's the people'. Neither side had the remotest idea of what the other was saying, but the pleasure of human contact shines through.

I will end with words from the past which say all this much better than I can: first, the precepts, 'Nothing too much' and 'Know Thyself' from the Oracle at Delphi, secondly the old Russian saying "ничего без труда не дается (nichevo bez truda ne dayotsya) - nothing is gained without hard work", and thirdly the famous saying by Christ, 'Love thy neighbour as thyself'.

www.ingramcontent.com/pod-product-compliance
Lightning Source LLC
Chambersburg PA
CBHW061406160426
42813CB00088B/2710